Creative
Flower Arranging

To Auntie Mo

Love

From

Mauri marilyn

and

Gordon

Christmas 1982.

X X

With love to Sarah,
our darling daughter-in-law
and mother of our first grandchild

Creative Flower Arranging

Violet Stevenson

Photography by Leslie Johns

Hamlyn
London · New York · Sydney · Toronto

Line illustrations by Ian Garrard
and Fiona Butler

This book is based on Violet Stevenson's
Flower Arrangement Cards first published in 1969

First published in this form in 1982 by
The Hamlyn Publishing Group Limited
London · New York · Sydney · Toronto

Filmset in England by Photocomp Ltd., Birmingham
in 11 on 12pt Bembo

Printed in Italy

ISBN 0 600 30525 2

Contents

Introduction

There is a world of difference between doing the flowers and making a flower arrangement. While many may be placidly content with the former, tens-of-thousands of men and women have found and continue to find a never ending joy and satisfaction in the latter. Those who have never stopped to consider the matter may wonder where lies the difference. From the purely practical point of view flower arrangement is a means of getting the full value for both the flowers and the time spent on preparing them for display, but aesthetically and psychologically it is much more than that, for it offers a valuable and fascinating means of self-expression and opportunities for creativity.

From being a pleasant domestic chore in the average home, flower arrangement has become a minor art form with devotees spread throughout the world, some of them banded together in a network of flower arrangement societies and garden clubs, others content to follow their practice at home. Converts are being made continually and it is to these that this book is mainly addressed. Some see flower arrangement as a substitute for painting, sculpture or embroidery. Of course, the basic materials the arranger uses to illustrate the forms or patterns in mind are themselves so wonderfully made that it is hardly possible to fail. It is true that these works of art are fleeting, but it is also true that the pleasure experienced – and sometimes the compliments they draw – compensate for their short lives and it is surprising how long the memory of a particularly pleasing flower arrangement will linger, bringing pleasure in retrospect sometimes for years.

Even when making a simple decoration for the home one has the opportunity to create exciting colour harmonies, to handle and appreciate textures perhaps hitherto unknown, to assess and even to influence shapes, to interpret moods, themes, events and seasons – yet these are only some of the enticements flower arrangement has to offer.

Materials

Materials are always at hand. One can be without flowers but one need never be without a flower arrangement, for in this context the term 'flower' is used in its widest sense. To the creative, every part of a plant which he or she considers appealing, exciting or decorative enough to be put on show is considered to be a flower. Thus we have leaves, fresh dried or skeletonised; embryo shoots; fruit, fruits, and vegetables; seed stems and seed vessels of all kinds; branches; plant skeletons; roots and root wood; driftwood; fungi; moss and lichen arranged alongside, or perhaps in place of, true flowers.

The true flowers may be bought, cheap or expensive, hothouse grown, imported, garden produced or they may be free, for weeds and wayside plants can, in the hands of the creative arranger, be made to look as lovely and as decorative as the choicest blooms.

If any or all of these should prove insufficient, there is no reason why other natural objects should not be presented with plant materials in a secondary role. Seashells, of which there is a diversity as fascinating as that of flowers; corals, rocks, pebbles, any other mineral which appeals, even coal, which I have seen used with pure white flowers in an alabaster bowl, are a few which come to mind and which are used in some of my own flower arrangements illustrated here.

These accessories are sometimes inspirational. They may perhaps prompt the idea for a pattern, a style, a colour harmony, a texture contrast or an association or atmosphere for a theme. Sometimes they add that touch of wonder which is the hallmark of a memorable flower arrangement. On the other hand, they can also be used for purely practical purposes. A large seashell or a group may, for instance, be used to mask a stem holder and to provide a source from which stems can be made to appear to rise.

Candles too play a similar role. When at times special colours sought for or even demanded are not provided generously enough by the flowers themselves, candles may be worth using. They come in such a variety of colours that it is seldom difficult to match them or harmonise them with the flowers. Candles are not necessarily intended to be lit. Often one or a group can be used to establish a centre point, an axis around which the arrangement can be built. This way they can save time as well as flowers and so can prove to be economic as well as distinctive. I suggest that flower arrangers will find it helpful to keep a store of candles of varying length, thickness and colour.

Containers

Those who are content merely to do the flowers usually have a very few conventional vases which are used time and time again in the same setting, but those who wish to create diverse styles and to use very varied materials as the year goes by, need a greater range. It is not essential to own a great number and my own stock is quite modest although I know arrangers who possess hundreds. You will no doubt notice that here and there throughout this book the same container appears as part of a different arrangement. You will notice also that not all the containers used were originally designed to hold flowers. Creative flower arrangers need to be as liberal here as elsewhere. Just as any plant material can be a flower if you wish it, so almost any vessel, if it has some quality which will suit your purpose, can be a container. There are so many objects about the home that can be brought into use. One thinks of trays, plates, mats, kitchen dishes, large ash trays, tankards, wine glasses, storage jars – and, in some cases, their tops. For certain types of arrangement

you can also use slices of wood, dried fungi, stone slabs or tiles; really, the range is limitless.

It does not matter that these may not be waterproof. Modern foamed plastics in which stems can be inserted so easily and held in place in a moist environment no matter at what angle, make it possible to use almost anything which appeals to the creative arranger. These, as is explained elsewhere, are easily protected so that their moisture does not seep out.

Having decided on what type of containers to collect, the arranger needs to know how best to care for the flowers which are to be displayed in them.

Conditioning

If your flower arrangements are to continue to look fresh and lovely for many days, it is important that you spend time before assembly in preparing them for their vase life. Almost all need to be conditioned in one way or another.

If you have to buy them or if you grow your own, bear in mind that most flowers should be gathered before they have reached their peak. They should mature and look their best *after* arrangement. Exceptions are most daisy-like flowers, pyrethrum and gerbera and some chrysanthemums for instance, which are best picked and bought when the outer ring of florets in the centre disc have opened. If these are too young they may not take water. Lilies and most other flowers grown from corms and bulbs can be cut as soon as the buds are coloured. These in fact offer less problems than any other flowers, for they appear to have no difficulty in 'drinking' and can be arranged right away after cutting, even in shallow water. Among these, gladioli, freesias and similar flowers should have no more than one of the lowest florets expanded if you are to get full value from them.

If you are uncertain as to the age of a flower, look for signs of pollen, stamens thickly encrusted or petals dusted with it. Not all pollen is yellow, poppy anemones for instance have a dusky blue pollen. This indicates that the flowers have already passed their peak.

A good florist will have flowers standing in deep, clean water and out of sun. Refuse any whose stems seem slimy and whose foliage is yellowing or perhaps grey and powdery or otherwise discoloured with mould. Like vegetables, fresh flowers should look crisp. If the weather is very cold, do not buy flowers or plants which have been displayed in the open air. If these have been greenhouse grown they become chilled and do not last well in water. See that the flowers and not just the damp stems are well covered before taking them out. It is prudent to carry a large, light, transparent plastic bag with you so that all can be enveloped in this before being carried out into the cold air.

Roses often disappoint more than any other bought flower because they are liable to droop at the neck and fail to open. These need conditioning well in the way explained later, but first ensure that the flowers are only just opening and that they are not too young. The sepals should already be turning away from the petals or laid back against the stem. Stems and leaves should feel firm and turgid.

If you grow your own flowers, cut everything early in the morning before the sun is playing fully on them and while the plants are still turgid after a cool and perhaps dewy night. Roses, however, are best picked after a few hours of sunshine, during which time they will have built up stores of essential sugar in their leaves.

If flowers are wet, carefully but firmly swish them back and forth in the air so that the water is shaken off and the blooms are dry before you take them indoors. This is a precaution. While some flowers might be all right, others, sweet peas and pansies for example, sometimes rot if they are left wet. Much depends upon the atmosphere in which they stand. Most flowers, especially soft-stemmed summer kinds, should be stood in water as soon as possible after they have been severed from the plant. Some flowers need a little help when they are being coaxed to take water. Floppy subjects such as scabious and leafy kinds such as forced tulips respond to

first being laid straight, then paper wrapped. Tall stems such as delphiniums can be rested against the sides of a bucket for support.

Use clean vessels and deep tepid water so that the level comes up to the necks of the blooms. Once they have had at least one hour under such conditions most flowers should be turgid enough to be arranged and they should continue to keep well charged with water. Some need longer and there are exceptions which need special treatment.

For instance, all members of the buttercup family, which includes clematis, delphiniums, paeony, anemone and ranunculus, are liable to wilt badly after arrangement if they have not been specially conditioned. Treat these and any unfamiliar flower, including hollyhocks, mallow and some wildings, in the same way as prescribed for all tough and woody stems. Ends of these should be split upwards for an inch or so, according to stem length, before being stood upright in boiling water deep enough to cover the split portion. Allow them to remain in the cooling water for some hours if necessary, until you can see that both flowers and leaves are crisp. Should any one appear to be wilting or even ready to wilt, repeat the process, making a fresh cut at the stem's base. Treat bought flowers the same. Stem ends of poppies, euphorbias (spurges) or any other exuding latex when cut should be held in a candle flame until charred.

A word of warning: it is often advised that you smash the stem ends of tough, fibrous or woody subjects with a hammer to expose the inner tissues. You may even buy flowers which have been treated this way. If so, cut off the smashed portion, make a new slit upwards as described before. Although the smashing certainly helps the stem to draw up water quickly, it has one great drawback. When fragments of those bruised and beaten tissues are released into the water they act in exactly the same way as immersed foliage, which means that they quickly rot and foul the water. A cut upwards through the centre of the base of the stem still exposes the water-conducting tissues, but is less likely to cause trouble because a smaller area is involved.

Some blossom branches wilt irretrievably, lilac and philadelphus are examples. In the first case simply cut away the laterals of young leaves from the flowering stem. Treat these and the flowering branches as described above, but separately. Both should quickly become turgid and once they are drinking well they should remain firm. If they should flag again repeat the process. Philadelphus usually wilts because it is carrying many leaves as well as petals and as moisture is given off from all of these, the total loss is great. It is wise always to cut away some of the foliage growing near or around shrub blossom in addition to that which is stripped off the stem ends.

Some flowers are likely to turn the water sour more quickly than others, gypsophila, pyrethrum, wallflowers and stocks come quickly to mind. All of these are types with very leafy stems. If the leaves remain on that part of stem which is to go under water, they will quickly rot and make the contents of the vessel offensive to you as well as to the flowers. So always take time to strip the stems of sappy, leafy flowers – it is not so important with evergreens and roses. Let the stems be as bare and as neat as possible and you will find that this also aids arrangement.

All vessels involved, for conditioning and for arrangement, should be scrupulously clean. This prevents excessive bacterial activity which results in the water turning sour, in effect becoming alive with an unwanted population. The commercial nutrients recommended as an aid for lasting freshness really do work. You can also use an aspirin or a copper penny. These last two act as inhibitors to bacteria. Metal containers have much the same influence. They also help to keep the water cool, just as beer is kept cool in a pewter tankard.

The various makes of foamed plastic stem holders contain substances which could be described as a disinfectant and so help to keep stem bases clean and the water sweet.

Nutrients also help to feed flowers. As an alternative, try a lump of sugar, a teaspoon of glucose or a saltspoon of honey to each pint of water. Feeding this way is most helpful in winter.

Be sure to keep glass vessels out of direct sunshine, for this playing on the water will quickly promote bacterial activity and you will see it becoming more and more opaque or discoloured.

Fresh materials for winter decoration need particular attention, for it is important to realise that at this time of year the environment in our homes is not really the ideal for cut flowers. Flowers which bloom out of doors in winter and early spring are more suited to low temperatures and cool, misty conditions. When they are moved into an artificially heated atmosphere the change is often too great.

The water
Once the decoration is in place it should receive some attention from time to time. All flowers drink most and fastest during the first hours after arrangement. It is then that you will discover that the water level has fallen considerably. Top it up with fresh water and continue to inspect it daily. When foamed plastic stem holders are used, ensure that these are kept constantly moist. Where possible cut the blocks a little less than the diameter of any vessel in which they are placed to allow space for a reservoir of water around them. Water evaporates very quickly from this foamed plastic, so pay especial attention to any which stand ex-container.

Where you know that flowers will not last for long, daffodils for instance, do not waste your time nor the flowers' efforts by changing the water constantly. Simply keep the level topped up daily. Where you have long-lasting materials such as chrysanthemums as well as foliage, carry out the daily topping-up and then, say once a fortnight, take the arrangement to the sink, tilt it gently to pour away the water without disturbing the arrangement. I usually do this from the back of the arrangement where I always leave a space between stem holder and rim to take the spout of a vase filler for topping up. Pour in more water at this point, allowing it to overflow and thus aerating it a little. Before returning it to its setting, tip out a little water so that this does not overspill and recharge the remainder with nutrient or plant food.

Sometimes you may be using flowers that just cannot strike the balance between the amount of water they can take up and the amount of moisture they lose. These include marigolds (calendula), polyanthus, hellebores, forget-me-nots, wallflowers and Brompton stocks. All of these should be arranged with at least two thirds of their stem length in water. You may find it best, as I do, to bunch these with their heads together, posy fashion, perhaps surrounded by an attractive and protective collar of leaves, and then, with their stems down in deep containers to treat them as one great bloom. It is quite easy to establish pleasant proportions if you arrange them this way. For instance, in a deep vase stand tall branches of early blossom at the back, a few daffodils before them with their stem ends only a little way down in the vase since these last best, as do most bulb flowers, in shallow water, and a full, collared posy of polyanthus at rim level. There are many variations to be played on this theme.

Stem holders
If you have turned the pages of this book and looked at some of the line drawings which explain how an arrangement has been assembled, you are sure to have noticed what an important role is played by the various stem holders which have been used in almost every arrangement illustrated.

The great difference between making a flower arrangement and merely putting some flowers in a vase of water is that in the first place you control the stems. You expect to be able to arrange them at some angle other than strictly upright and that the flowers will stay in place even when jostled by other flowers as they in turn are arranged.

Through the years there have been many introductions of specially designed stem holders, such as domes of glass full of holes for stems, or a single layer of metal mesh to lay across the top of a bowl or vase, but none of

these proved to be really efficient. All had drawbacks of some form or another. It was not until wire netting was shown to be most effective that flower arrangement became something that anyone could enjoy.

This common material is still one of the best, and certainly one of the cheapest, of all stem holders. It is important that the mesh should be large, $1\frac{1}{2}$ to 2 in (4 to 5 cm), even when used for small containers. Only this kind is malleable and can be squeezed into any shape or pushed into any aperture. Even when crumpled tightly it will still give way sufficiently to accommodate a thick stem as it passes down through the netting. It is virtually everlasting. The most practical thing to do is to cut pieces to fit each container you use. To store them, wash them with the vessel after the flowers are dissembled and replace the dry netting in the clean container ready for use again at some future date.

You can get by on wire netting alone because it can be adapted to any style or purpose, but even more versatile is the foamed plastic marketed in convenient blocks of various sizes and shapes. This is not so cheap nor long lasting as wire netting, but any arranger will find it invaluable, especially for gift arrangements or others which have to be transported. Even when well soaked with water and heavy, it retains its shape as stems are pushed into it. This means that it is not essential to place it inside a vessel. For instance, you can use a flat plate as a container. Specially designed plastic holders to retain these plastic shapes can be bought quite cheaply and these can be used on their own or placed inside another more attractive but perhaps less water-tight object. Large blocks can be cut easily with a long knife.

Another advantage is that this type of stem holder will retain flowers quite securely no matter at what angle their stems have been inserted. It is not necessary either always to insert a long portion of stem. Depending upon the weight of the bloom, sometimes this can be as short as $\frac{1}{2}$ in (1 cm) or so. This means that many large flowers with short stems, cluster roses for instance, can be used so much more effectively than when their stems have to reach down to the water held inside a vessel. For instance, blocks cut to protrude above the rim level of a deep container can hold large short-stemmed flowers for the focal point of an arrangement.

Unfortunately this plastic has a limited life because it becomes pitted after use and finally disintegrates. Sometimes, for the second time of use, it is possible simply to turn the block upside down when it will look and behave almost like new. You can also press used pieces to compact them slightly and then place a new slice on top. Crumbled pieces covered with a new top can be used to fill deep containers, especially if these are to hold long stems. Small or crumbled pieces can be held together in a plastic net bag and used as a unit. Ideally, once made moist this plastic should be kept moist, even when in store.

This kind of plastic, which has a fairly soft surface, can also be used dry for dried flower arrangements. It is to be especially recommended for fragile dried stems, which enter it easily. Where these are mounted on wires, or where tough or woody stems are to be arranged, another kind of much firmer plastic, which is not water absorbent nor retentive, can be used. This kind is also marketed in a variety of shapes and sizes, greater in fact than the first.

Generally speaking blocks of foamed plastic can be used in ways once exclusively limited to heavy metal pin holders, which incidentally have been employed for centuries in Japanese flower arrangement. However, these pin holders, like wire netting, are extremely durable and although perhaps expensive in the first place, may prove to be the best buy for some people. They vary from very tiny examples, some of which lock together to make a larger unit, to wide, heavy holders 3 or 4 in (8 or 10 cm) across. Some pin holders are made of materials other than all metal, but the lighter they are in weight the less efficient they are likely to be.

All pin holders should be well anchored to the surface on which they stand. Generally three or four pea-sized pills of plasticine or adhesive clay applied to bone dry surfaces are sufficient to hold them securely in place. Roll the pills, press them lightly on the underside of the pin holder, then press this down hard on the floor of the container. It should then stick fast.

Sometimes it is helpful to combine two or more kinds of stem holder when the ingredients for an arrangement are mixed. Some pin holders have finer points than others. Frail stems are not easily impaled upon thick points, neither are very fleshy stems. It is helpful in such cases to combine a ball of squeezed wire netting with a pin holder, placed at this point where the fine stemmed flowers are to be arranged. This can be hooked to the edge of the holder as well as on it at the centre or to one side or another. Alternatively, if the fine stems are not also soft, a small block of foamed plastic can be used in much the same way. Sometimes all three kinds of stem holders can be used together.

Wire netting is easily cut with the right tools. Best are florist scissors, the kind used by professionals, made of strong steel with a notch low down the blades to take wire. An old pair of secateurs can also be used for this purpose, but spare your good gardening pairs. Use these instead to cut all woody stems. Ordinary or kitchen scissors tend to nip the stems and can even prevent them from taking up water easily.

Readers tell me that they often have difficulty in buying florist wires from florists. Many garden centres sell small bundles of these as well as reel wire and florist tape along with foamed plastic and other items mentioned above.

Even if you do not intend to resort to floristry proper, a few wires near at hand are often extremely helpful, not only to use as false stems and to elongate some short stem, but also to repair and save a flower where the hollow stem has become bent or damaged in some way. A wire passed up internally through the stem to a point beyond the damaged area will help it to last as well as others of its kind.

Simple Beginnings

There are just a few flowers – very few really – which appear to be complete in themselves when stood in water. A rose is an example. In its case, not only the intricately petalled bloom, but also its glossy leaves and characteristic thorns bring the total sum to beauty, especially if the flower stands in a slim glass vase through which the silky stem and thorns are magnified. We can then closely admire the smooth textures of the one and the contrasting precise shapes and often brilliant colour of the other.

To display a solitary rose this way is arrangement of a kind, but one could not claim that it is creative in any way. The majority of flowers, which are less complete than the rose, call for more ingenuity if we hope to gain full value and pleasure from them as decorations. This is certainly the case when for some reason there are only few flowers available.

Those who are new to flower arrangement can learn so much by beginning simply, by taking just a few, even one, two or three flowers (try dividing a bunch of ten into three or more lots) and devising ways and means of making them appear to be of greater consequence than they really are.

Sometimes the flower's own plant, like the rose, offers sufficient material to complement the blooms. There may be an abundance of foliage, or perhaps seedheads or fruits, even stem ends such as you see on page 00, but most often one needs to search for other items. Some of these are long lasting and can be stored to be used time and time again.

Foliage can be used to frame the flowers as well as to provide contrasts of texture, colour and shape. Graceful branches of foliage or tall, slim, spicate or grass-like leaves, seed stems and many kinds of fruits can be used to add height and width when flowers are short stemmed. These subjects also bring substance to an arrangement.

Many flowers are leafless, or almost so. Often leaves from some other plant will complement them beautifully. Chunky driftwood, gnarled bark, pebbles, raw glass, attractive stones, coral, large leaves will also furnish arrangements, either alone or in concert. At the same time, these serve a practical purpose and hide stem holders from view.

Not the least important part of arrangements of this type are their containers. When only few flowers are to be used these are not likely to be as concealed as they are when they hold a mass. They should be in tune both with the materials they support and the styles in which these are arranged.

Spring Scene – *three lily-flowered tulips and a branch of harmonising apple blossom create a simple yet colourful decoration*

Winter Greeting

To greet the year, five snowdrops with the first catkins and a few evergreen ivy leaves as a foil

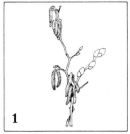

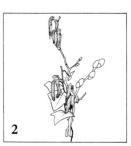

1 The easiest way to arrange any flowers in a narrow-necked container of any size is to tie most of the materials, sometimes all of them, together first, like these snowdrops, hazel catkins and willow. Gauge the height of the arrangement. The tallest, measured from the rim, should be at least one-and-a-half times the height of the container.

2 The ivy leaves are added not only to help to hide the tie but, so long as the stems are left long enough, to flow out over the top of the vase prettily. This method also applies to blooms, other materials and containers which are much larger than those used here.

3 Place the bunch in the vase and adjust it so that the catkins droop gracefully and the leaves flow out in such a way that the little snowdrops will look as though they are rising up from them. Sometimes the stem ends need shortening or levelling so that the bunch 'sits' well in the container.

18

Simple Elegance

Paeonies with copper beech

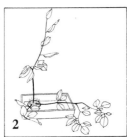

1 Fresh copper beech has been used here, but preserved branches of other foliage can be arranged in the same way. These last for several years and can be used time and time again. Fix a pinholder firmly to the base of a flower trough or attractive gratin dish to hold the sprays in place.

2 Arrange a tall branch to form the apex of a rough triangle with the two side stems flowing out from the holder in different directions. Prune away damaged and overlapping leaves to give a neat and slender outline. Slit or slant stem ends so that they can be easily impaled on the pinholder.

3 Let the paeonies follow the line of the stems, but shorten them so that they lie within the framework of leaves. Follow the same theme as the branches, with the tallest, medium and shortest flowers flowing alongside the appropriate stem. Later, hide the pinholder with surplus clusters of leaves.

Simplicity

Paeonies with their own foliage

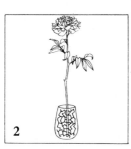

1 Paeonies should be bought or cut in bud so that they open slowly in water. This way they are more entertaining and will last longer. Fill the vase from base to rim with large mesh wire-netting, but in this case, keep the ends just below rim level so that the stems rise neatly and apparently without aid.

2 Remove any large leaves from the stems, but see that some of the upper leaves are retained otherwise much of the character of the flowers will be lost. Arrange the tallest stem in a vertical position, making sure that it is firmly held in the netting and cannot move later.

3 Arrange the shorter second stem so that it leans away from the centre stem leaving a space roughly the diameter of the flower between the two. Place the largest bloom (or bud) lowest in the arrangement. The length of its stem above rim level should be roughly equal to the height of the container. Then arrange extra leaves.

Wood Nymph

Three carnations in a modern trough form a pleasing pattern which can be used on any day of the year

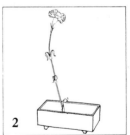

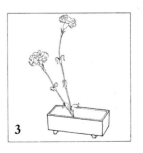

1 Use rectangular pinholder and place it to the left of the container. Press plasticine or adhesive clay pills lightly on the dry base of the pinholder, then press them firmly to the dry floor of the container. This will hold the pinholder securely in position.

2 The fullest carnation stem should be as long as the length plus the height of the container and half as much again. Arrange it at an angle of about ten degrees from the vertical. Try to face the flower so that it looks inwards.

3 The second stem should be three-quarters the length of the first stem. Impale it on the pinholder so that its lower stem flows the same way as that of the first flower. Try to make it look towards the tallest flower. The third stem should be half the length of the second and arranged on the pinholder so the bloom lies between the two taller stems facing upwards. Flowing pieces of driftwood are finally placed at the base of the arrangement.

Flower Patterns

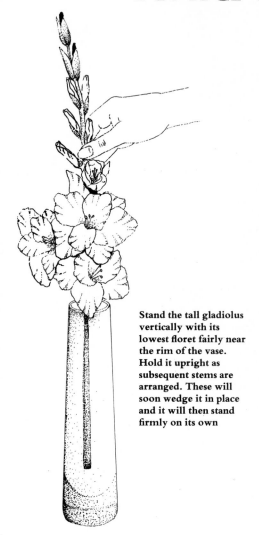

Stand the tall gladiolus vertically with its lowest floret fairly near the rim of the vase. Hold it upright as subsequent stems are arranged. These will soon wedge it in place and it will then stand firmly on its own

Some flowers are more complex than the single bloom supported on an unbranching stem. These can be a source of inspiration, for they offer the arranger the basis of unusual and attractive decorations. An arrangement which uses one important flower as the major portion can be very simple indeed and takes very little time or trouble, yet the results can be quite exciting. The secret is to have everything in harmony.

Flowers such as the gladiolus illustrated here provide a wonderful area of colour as well as delightful shape, floral pattern and texture. Their self colours can be found in so many of the simple plant materials which grow all around us. Alternatively, one can turn to complementary and contrasting colour harmonies, which are described later.

In this arrangement trails of Virginia creeper from the wall of the house were prettily touched with tints of the same lovely crimson of the flower. They also provide contrast of both shape and character, the little trails bringing a note of frivolity to the stolid flower spike.

The flowers on a gladiolus stem fade from the base upwards. So that this particular arrangement should continue to look good for several days, a full round head of harmonising hydrangea was arranged at rim level; actually, this also serves other purposes. Its dense shape anchors the tall gladiolus to the slim container. It helps to widen the shape of the arrangement at rim level and so prevents it from appearing top heavy. The large leaves of the creeper, also arranged low down, correct the balance. At first the hydrangea is partly hidden by the lowest gladiolus flowers, but as these fade and are removed it will come into its own.

The tall stems of orach arranged behind the gladiolus bring more contrast of shape and texture and help furnish the arrangement. A branch of some small-foliaged plant or of berries would have a similar effect.

The brown of the container, a 'broken' colour made of red and green blends pleasingly. It is heavy enough to stand securely in spite of the height of the flowers it holds. Yet at its rim it is slim enough to take their few thick stems without the need of a stem holder which might mar the effect if seen through the glass.

One lovely gladiolus forms the major part of this colourful arrangement held in a slim glass vase.

Old Pewter

Cupressus with chrysanthemums in a pewter tankard

1 Flowers last longer in metal containers than in other vessels because they retard bacterial activity in the water thus keeping it sweet. Fill the tankard with large mesh wire-netting keeping the ends fanned out at the back. If stems are thick or heavy, hook cut ends of netting round the handle.

2 Chrysanthemums last a very long time but their leaves fade faster than their petals. For this reason, make a framework of harmonising foliage that will live longer. Flat-growing branches make a good frame. Here, the cupressus matches the pewter. Trim and lighten the branch tips.

3 Mass-produced flowers tend to be both perfect and uniform and to fall into geometric patterns when arranged. The lacy background of foliage softens these. Strip flower stem ends of leaves to keep water clean. Arrange the tallest stem first. Its tip should be roughly in line with the handle. Then arrange the other blooms so that each is well displayed.

Leaf Sculpture

Copper beech with vallota lilies. Preserved beech can be used in this way in winter with any bulb flowers

1 The tallest stem should measure one-and-a-half times the combined length of the width and the height of the container. Place this in position on a small pinholder first. Make sure that it stands firm.

2 The second stem should measure roughly three-quarters the total length of the tallest stem. Try to make the stems appear to rise up from the pinholder together as though they were growing. The third stem should be roughly three-quarters the length of the second stem.

3 To give an air of delicacy many of the leaves need removing. Begin first with any which are damaged by weather or insects. Then remove overlapping leaves in such a way that any line upwards or downwards is accentuated. Do not remove so many that the character of the plant is lost. Finally insert the three flowers and hide the pinholder with a carefully placed piece of wood or some other object, such as an attractive stone.

Gentle Flutter

Summer cornus, or dogwood, with chincherinchees in a pattern which can be repeated in early spring with forced branches

1 Press plasticine or adhesive clay pills on the base of a dry pinholder and press on to the dry base of the bowl. Add water when the arrangement is completed. Dogwood stems are supple and their branches can be coaxed to curve a little more by shaping them in the hand before arrangement.

2 Slant or split the ends of branches so that they are easily impaled on the points of the pinholder. Curve the ends of the dogwood so that all three main stems can rise up from the container together before each goes its separate way.

3 Cut away all leafless side stems. Remove any damaged or insect-eaten leaves. Remove one or more leaves if these hide the flower blossom so that this is clearly visible. Later, when the chincherinchees are arranged, keep these shorter than the shortest dogwood stem. Freesias may be used as an alternative.

Simple Luxury

Marbled arum leaves and lady's slipper orchids, or cypripediums, arranged with sprays of willow

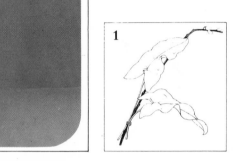

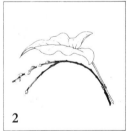

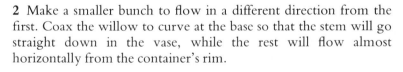

1 When very narrow-necked containers are used, different methods of arrangement have to be employed. As we have seen, it is often best to bunch and tie some of the materials first and then to arrange them as one stem. If necessary, coax the willow to curve more by bending it in the hands.

2 Make a smaller bunch to flow in a different direction from the first. Coax the willow to curve at the base so that the stem will go straight down in the vase, while the rest will flow almost horizontally from the container's rim.

3 Place the two bunches in the vase. Make sure that the stem ends are in sufficient water. Gently pull the arum leaves into position so tht they face you and show their beautiful markings. The orchids are best arranged one by one. Single sprays of flowers may also be effectively displayed this way.

Patterns
of the West

Even flowers which are arranged quite casually with no predetermined style of arrangement in mind tend to fall into a pattern. This is really quite logical when one considers that by differing the stem length of each flower so that every bloom is given space to display itself, or as in many cases, to continue to grow, each flower will be above, below or to one side of another.

If you were to take any of the pictures in this book and then describe an outline, real or imaginary, so as to link the tips of the tallest, longest or lowest of the flowers in it, you would find that the arrangement is bounded, admittedly sometimes roughly, by the shape of a triangle of some kind, not necessarily on a horizontal base. Or the shape could be a semi- or part-circle, oval or part- or half-oval.

In this chapter we look at some of the more formal of these patterns, in particular at those in which many flowers are used.

Consider flowers which may be required to decorate a table. This arrangement will be viewed from all angles, even from above should it be placed on a low table. It follows, therefore, that it would be best to make it as symmetrical as possible, with the opposite sides at least equal or matching, or better still perhaps, with the decoration appearing to be the same shape from whatever angle it is viewed. The chosen style will really depend

Summer Glory – *in traditional style, vivid blue borage from the herb border mingles with hollyhocks, sweet peas and roses.*

upon both the setting and the purpose of the flower decoration.

Or take flowers which may be required to play the role of a focal point, or the major decoration in some other area of a room, the arrangement standing perhaps on a chest, side table or pedestal. This will be seen from a different viewpoint. In this case there is no need to waste any of the precious flowers by placing them where they are likely to be hidden from view. It is possible to fill a vessel in such a way that the unseen area, the back of the arrangement, is almost flat against the wall. In a way such arrangements resemble a peacock's tail, spread out and beautiful, but with all the components gradually leaning further and further forward until near rim level the flowers reach out into the room.

Both these styles follow the most popular and useful patterns of the West. They are based on the shapes and characters of the traditional posy and sheaf used in many countries for centuries. At one time the flowers in both posy and sheaf would have been first bunched, the first surrounded by a collar of fern fronds or other foliage, the other backed by the same, and then stood in water. For centuries vases were designed to take these heavy bunches and to hold them securely, which is why so many old vases have a wide base and a slim waist.

As you would expect, through the years and because of so many varied influences, these two styles have become adapted so that now they can be designed to suit modern settings and interiors, modern containers and, not the least important, modern flowers.

The original posy was dome-shaped, sometimes cone-like. 'All-round' arrangements, that is those which can be viewed from any angle and will appear much the same to the uncritical eye, usually follow the same shape. Obviously it is possible to play many variations on this theme, which is where the creativity of flower arrangement comes into its own. However, because the style is so formal it is possible to give a few hard and fast rules which can be followed at the outset of assembly to ensure success. Even when many flowers are to be used these formal symmetrical arrangements really are quite easy to assemble if you go about them the right way.

The most important piece is the central one. Here it is wise to place the straightest stemmed flower, or whatever else you may use, such as a grass, a leafy branch or seed stem. If none of the stems you have are really straight, then handle and rearrange the material until its bloom or tip is directly in the centre.

This central stem in a way forms an axis and once it is established it is really quite easy to arrange all other stems in relation to it. The important factor is that all other parts of the arrangement, all other stems, should lean away from this central stem, to a lesser degree if nearly as tall and sited near it, or to a greater degree if they are larger, wider, heavier or denser, in which case they should go lower in the arrangement.

If all stems are made to appear as though they have sprung from the foot of this central stem a pleasant effect of natural growth and unity is achieved. To obtain this effect, simply point the base of every stem you are about to arrange to the centre, even if in reality it is to be placed just inside the rim.

To strike the correct balance, wherever possible the bloom at the centre (when a flower is used in this role) should also be smaller than or at least the same size as those surrounding it. It should never be much larger. Unfortunately, so often the flowers with the longest stems carry the largest

flowers. Where mixtures of flowers are to be arranged there are ways of correcting the balance, as we shall see later.

Having placed a vertical stem in position, or one which will appear to be vertical when all are arranged, the next step is to define the width of the arrangement. This is best done by placing side stems at right angles, or roughly so, to the centre stem. These can be flowers, trails of foliage or other materials. The line drawings provided with the arrangements in this chapter show many examples of this procedure. Other more pendent stems can be arranged later to eliminate stiffness and formality of pattern.

These side stems are also important in that they define the shape and can guide you as to what pattern to follow. For instance, should they be much shorter than the central stem it follows that the arrangement will be fairly compact. If they are much longer, then the arrangement will, of course, be much more spreading.

The intermediate stems placed between the central and side stems help to sketch the outline of the design, that is, whether it is to be based on a half or part globe, an oval or on a cone.

If the arrangement is to be viewed on all sides, one must ensure that all the flowers are evenly distributed. To do this follow the procedures just described, then give the vessel a half turn and repeat the process, placing side and intermediate stems in position. After this arrange two or three flowers in one area then similar flowers in the area opposite, turning the vessel rather than walking around the arrangement, unless, of course, this is to be on a very large scale.

As assembly takes place distribute the flowers and other materials carefully, sharing them out as evenly as possible. When one is put in place match it on the opposite side. Never try to arrange all the flowers on one side of the arrangement and then turn your attention to the other. This never works successfully. Large leaves cut from stems which have to be shortened can be left on the trimmed main stem and arranged low to flow prettily over the rim, to frame flowers and to help hide the stemholder. Some blooms can be recessed among slightly longer stemmed flowers so that the surface of the arrangement is prettily contoured.

When arrangements based on the sheaf style are to be assembled, much the same rules apply, but the vessel does not have to be turned. In the initial stages the great difference is that while the central stem still plays the same role, it should no longer occupy the very centre of the vessel. Instead it should go as far back against the rim as possible. This ensures that enough space is left for the other flowers.

Once the centre, side and intermediate stems have been arranged, begin arranging the taller ones from the centre downwards. These should lean forwards very slightly at first until, when the rim is reached, some will flow out over it and even below according to the nature of the arrangement and the materials used.

Again, do not try to complete one area before beginning on another. Matching is not so important here as balancing the materials. For instance, when using a mixture and only one large bloom is available, if this goes on one side of the centre it may be necessary to arrange several small ones on the other side to compensate. Where the flowers are uniform, stems have to be shortened carefully so that each bloom has its own display space.

Silver Wedding

*Peach Blossom tulips and
Roman hyacinths with
Sterling Silver roses*

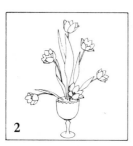

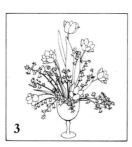

1 The tulips could be replaced by other flowers or by more Sterling Silver roses. It is nice to make an arrangement containing some of the recipient's favourite flowers and to add the roses because of their name. If the arrangement has to be transported, use some foamed plastic stem holder, but for static arrangements wire-netting can be used.

2 Begin at the back of the vase by placing the tallest stem in position as near to the rim as possible. When arranging the other flowers point their stems towards the base of the tallest one. Gradually 'sketch' in the outline of the arrangement with the tallest stems.

3 Group the same kind of flowers together but do not make this zoning too rigid. Give each one space to expand and to be seen to advantage. Let some of the lowest flowers lean right out over the rim of the vase. Add the roses last of all. Obviously, a silver container could be used.

Burst of Spring

Forced guelder rose (virburnum) contrasting with stiff-stemmed gladioli, tulips, irises and buttercups, cabbage flowers and doronicum

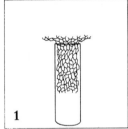

1 Cut a piece of wire-netting twice the height of the vase and a little wider. Fold it into a U shape. Arrange with cut ends well above the rim and pull out to support lower stems. The water will add weight to the vase.

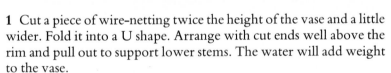

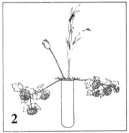

2 If the tips of stems are turned to left or right rather than to the front, even the stiffest ones become more graceful. Cut or buy gladioli 'hard', that is with the lower flower just showing colour, and tulips and iris in bud or just opening. Strip leaves from stem ends to lessen bulk.

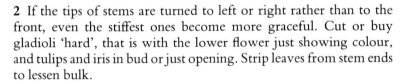

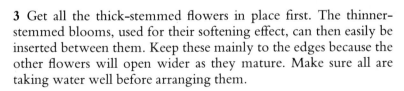

3 Get all the thick-stemmed flowers in place first. The thinner-stemmed blooms, used for their softening effect, can then easily be inserted between them. Keep these mainly to the edges because the other flowers will open wider as they mature. Make sure all are taking water well before arranging them.

Country Gardens

Viburnum, early delphiniums, alstroemeria, euphorbia and marguerites

1 Throughout spring and summer blossom can be used to make a glorious background to other flowers. Fill a pedestal vase with a block of well-soaked foamed plastic or, alternatively, use wire-netting. Arrange the tallest stem of the viburnum so that its tip is over the centre of the base of the container.

2 Trim the centre stem so that its branches flow only to the left and the right. Any prunings can be arranged lower down. The lateral stems define the width of the arrangement. Where possible, select curved stems or cut these so that a side branch retains a portion of the main stem.

3 Arrange the other flowers in rough groups, rather as they would grow in a border. Use spicate shapes, such as delphiniums, at the edges of an arrangement. Let all the other stems lean at an angle away from the central tallest viburnum branch.

Good Companions

Pyrethrums are long lasting. Let them stay as originally arranged while the more fleeting sweet peas are replaced

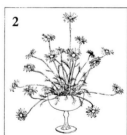

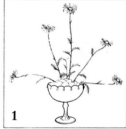

1 Thoroughly soak foamed plastic in water. Make a parcel of it with wire-netting to fill the vase; it will not matter if it crumbles. Be sure to strip the part of pyrethrum stem which goes into the stem holder but keep the leaves on as low as possible so that they help to hide it.

2 Place the first stems of pyrethrum to be arranged as near to the back of the vase as possible. If they have to be shortened, reserve the pieces which are cut away, strip ends and trim where necessary, and arrange them low among the stems to provide foliage and to cover the stem holder.

3 All stems should be arranged at an angle flowing from the base of the tallest. This should be the only vertical, or positioned as near vertical as possible. Let some of the stems flow forward and out from the centre to give a third dimension, but also recess some to give depth and shade.

Wayside Beauties

Arrangements which call for masses of flowers need never be expensive and they will be none the less beautiful because of this. There are so many lovely plant materials around us, on waysides, on waste ground, or even in our own gardens which might so easily be passed over and yet which can be made to look so lovely, even elegant, when arranged. This is not to suggest that wild flowers should be gathered indiscriminately, the precious ones should be left to bloom and seed, but there are others which are so plentiful that no one will scold should they be gathered.

All green, green and white or green and yellow colour schemes for flowers are always appealing and very easy to create. Throughout the year one can find plenty of garden and wayside materials which are decorative enough to be used on their own or to supplement garden or bought flowers.

Where cow parsley cannot be found there are other garden plants with similar kinds of flowers, chervil, parsley, coriander, caraway, fennel and dill, for example. On the other hand, bought and usually cheap gypsophila, that much abused flower, can be made to look both elegant and unusual arranged in this manner.

White dead nettle has no real counterpart among the cultivars, although it is common enough as a weed. The nearest cultivated flower to it in shape and character is the apple-green moluccella or shell flower. Like the latter the wilding's stems curve obligingly when the flowers are stood in water. In both flowers it is necessary to cut away most of the foliage so that the whorls of florets can be seen in their full beauty.

In this arrangement garden-grown wood spurge helps fill in the outline and contributes to the general pattern. Most of the spurges or euphorbias are highly decorative and last well when cut.

When a lateral has to be cut from a main stem see that a portion of this main stem is still attached. This is always at an angle to the lateral which means that when it is pushed down into the container the lateral will flow out at an attractive and easy angle

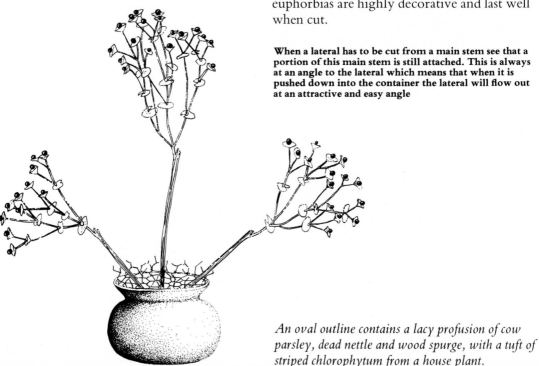

An oval outline contains a lacy profusion of cow parsley, dead nettle and wood spurge, with a tuft of striped chlorophytum from a house plant.

Summer Pattern

An assortment of little annuals with lavender, roses, coloured leaves, pinks and perennial daisies

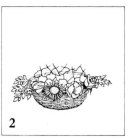

1 Line a little basket with polythene or cooking foil. Alternatively, use a shallow bowl. If the polythene is thin, use it double or triple thickness. Test that it is quite waterproof. Turn the edges of this lining back inside the basket so that it does not show or, alternatively, trim level with scissors.

2 Fill with well-soaked foamed plastic topped with a little wire-netting. Make certain that this does not pierce the lining. Cut ends can be hooked over the edges of the basket if necessary. Arrange little flowers and leaves round the rim so that both the polythene lining and stem holder are hidden.

3 Next place the tallest of the flowers in position in the centre. Strip the portion of stem which will go under water as arrangement takes place. This makes them easier to insert into any stem holder, and also keeps the water sweeter for a longer time. Mass the flowers quite thickly. Short-stemmed flowers can be used effectively this way.

Garnet Red

Garnette and Carole roses in a wine glass

1 Although they are extremely long-lasting, Garnette and Carole roses are smaller than most other shop roses and so a dainty container suits them. A large rose-coloured wine glass is ideal. Push a mass of black plastic-covered wire-netting into the mouth of the glass. Secure it by hooking an end or two over the rim. Alternatively, use a block of foamed plastic.

2 Arrange the tallest stem through the centre of the stem holder, setting it near the back of the glass to allow space for the other roses. Strip leaves from the portion to go under water but keep as many on the lower part of the stem as possible. Roses need plenty of foliage to feed the blooms.

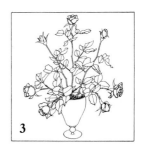

3 Treat the remaining stems in the same way, retaining as much foliage as possible without making the arrangement appear dense and heavy. Later, you can arrange some leaves low down to hide the rim and stem holder from sight.

Lessons
from the East

The types of flower arrangements discussed in the previous chapter can be made and have been made throughout the centuries because there never has been a lack of plant materials in the West. Even in winter it is possible to find something decorative, be it no more than evergreen ivy and holly with their attendant berries. Even so, these are not the base of everyday flower decorations, for not everyone enjoys massive arrangements, besides which they do not suit every setting nor every occasion. In recent years arrangers have turned more and more to oriental styles in which fewer flowers are employed.

These offer a much wider scope for creativity. To return to our winter ivy and holly cited above, a few carefully placed trails of the former grouped perhaps with a few skeletal seedstems and a mossy stone or two is much more likely to stir the senses than a heap of glossy green leaves. Apart from the atmosphere such arrangements can evoke, another factor plays an important part. Simple arrangements also offer you a truly economic way of decorating a room and how satisfying to find that by saving pennies you can also create beauty – fleeting beauty perhaps, but often truly memorable just the same.

In many areas of the East, especially in the tropics, surprisingly perhaps, flowers can be scarce and even those which are abundant

Prettily variegated cabbages, garrya catkins and arbutus fruits arranged in the oriental manner. To the creative flower arranger all lovely plant materials are flowers

have poor lasting qualities. It is probably this factor which originally had the greatest influence on the basically similar styles which have evolved in that part of the world. There are many and different schools of oriental flower arrangement. However, the styles which have had the greatest universal influence on modern arrangement are derived from the ancient school of traditional Japanese flower arrangement which was first practised many centuries ago. Changes have occurred from time to time as new attitudes were adopted until today there are many schools, each with its own interpretation of the original conception of the ancient masters. However, the fundamental principles still underlie this style as they underlie the greatly differing western patterns of arrangement. What has happened also is that there has been a marriage between eastern and western flower arrangement where we see the mass and colour of the one blended with the simple lines of the other, but more of this later.

Just as it is difficult to follow one's own country's cooking if you live in a foreign land, so I suggest it is difficult to follow strictly the rules for Japanese flower arrangement if you live in the West and like to have western things around you. On the other hand, the rules which govern this particular style of arrangement are so helpful and so conducive to creativity that I feel it is well worth while conforming to them if only for a brief practising period. Study of this kind will prove to be very rewarding. Once you become skilled, both eyes and senses become quick to detect what will or will not be pleasing or harmonious. Having followed the rules until they become almost second nature, you can then bend them to suit your own tastes, to create your own style and perhaps to found your own school.

True Japanese flower arrangement is accompanied by much ritual, which is understandable since its ancient origins lie in religion. However, underlying the sophisticated interpretations of this art are many simple and very practical laws. I suggest that unless you wish to study oriental flower arrangement seriously, you respectfully brush aside the hallowed trappings and study the more earthly basics of this particular aspect of flower arrangement.

The examples illustrated in this chapter are all based on the principles which govern the ancient rules, but they do not follow them strictly. They are a compromise between hard and fast rules and informality. In order to show how effectively a few blooms can be displayed, they are my interpretations of Japanese styles and thus the arrangements have become personalised. Although it is possible to buy all kinds of oriental containers and accessories, these arrangements use containers and other objects which are to be found about the home. They also contain western flowers and garden materials.

As we have seen, there are no special names for the central, side and intermediate stems described in the previous chapter which deals with traditional western arrangements, but there are special names for the important stems used in the traditional Japanese styles. Basically the old flower masters taught that an arrangement should consist of three main principles or main lines of design. They considered and taught that these were symbolic of Heaven – *Shin*, Earth – *Soe*, and with Man – *Hikae*, as the link between the two. These three main stems, known as *Sushi*, are always arranged in such a manner that they form an irregular triangle.

More than the three stems can be used in this style of arrangement and when they are they should always be placed within the outline of the triangle made by the three principals so that they are submissive to them. These additional stems are known as *Jushi*.

As in all flower arrangements, proportions are of great importance and for these Japanese styles hard and fast rules are laid down. These are worth studying because they can be applied to so many other styles with pleasing results. The chosen container offers the guide to the length of the stems. When a tall vessel is used, the longest stem should be at least one and a half times as tall as the container plus its width. The opposite is required for a wide vessel, in which case the tallest stem should measure one and a half times the width plus the depth. Measurements are taken from the rim of the vessel. The tallest stem can be much taller than this, but it should never be shorter. (It is worth experimenting and both following and challenging this concept so that the eye can judge the validity of this rule.) The tallest stem should be put in place first of all. The second tallest, which should always be placed to one side of the first, should be roughly three quarters the length of the tallest. The shortest, the third stem, should in turn be three quarters the length of the second stem. This stem is considered to be the lowly one and should always flow forward away from the others.

After proportions, it is the placement of the stems which influence both the style and the effect of the finished arrangement. The rule here is the rule which can be followed profitably in every other style of arrangement – that each stem should lean a little way from the others. It is also important that stems rise, or appear to rise as one from the mouth of a tall container or from the same point in a wide or shallow one.

We have seen that in western style arrangements it is also important that one creates this effect of materials springing or rising from one point, but where many flowers are massed it is not essential that the stems should all be seen as coming from one source, only that one creates that impression. However, where few stems are used it is important that the effect is visual, because without it the arrangement has no unity.

In oriental styles the tallest stem plays an important role and because purity of line is essential it is usually vital to spend time and thought on its placement. The old rule decrees that the tip of the tallest curved stem should always be directly over the centre of the container, or the base of the object on which the container stands, even if this be a mat should this project well beyond the container's base and considered to be a part of the composition.

As you would expect, there is much more to Japanese arrangement than the placement of three or more stems. There are rules about many other aspects, for instance that an arrangement should always stand on a base, that the water plays an important part since it is symbolic of the soil from which all plants spring, that branch tips must always look up and never down as they grow naturally, that the third stem although lowly should never assume a drooping posture, neither should it

ever be allowed to lie in the water, to mention only a few. Although these may appear to be esoteric these rules are the results of lessons once learned from practical observation and experience and still deserve to be adopted by the practical minded arranger. For instance, leafy or woolly stems which trail in water can cause a siphon and so empty a vessel of water. Moisture from a container stood on a base of some kind is less likely to damage the surface of the table on which it stands.

There is another important lesson which can be learned by all those who are new to the art of flower arrangement. In the Japanese language the word *Hana* which we translate as 'flower' includes all manner of natural materials. Branches of blossom, foliage and berries, stems, branches, even parts of flowerless trees and shrubs, driftwood, lichened growth, fungi anything in fact that forms or once formed part of a plant can be considered a 'flower' and used to create a floral picture.

Meditation

Two arums, a leaf and driftwood. Use wild arums in spring or two daffodils and a dieffenbachia leaf

1 Curving stems need to be well anchored. Spend time at the beginning to ensure that the stem is quite firm. Creeper stems, bare wisteria or ivy for example can be used as an alternative to driftwood. For good balance try to get the tip of the stem over the centre of the base of the container.

2 The tallest arum leans out from the base of the curving wood as though it were growing within its boundary. Because the wood is so curved the arum's line is not accentuated, but it is important that all stems rise from the same point or appear to do so.

3 An arum leaf is the third important component in this arrangement. It flows the same way as the flower and cuts across the curving line of the wood. Later, the shorter arum and the other piece of wood will carry on this line to form an arc.

Serenity

Irises are available for arrangement during many months of the year according to their kind and season

1

1 Small pinholders of varying sizes are suitable for an arrangement like this. Alternatively, small, heavy holders made from plumber's lead can be shaped into a small ring just large enough to hold a stem.

2 The three important stems are separated in this arrangement. The first and second go onto the left-hand pinholder, the third on the right-hand pinholder. The tall first stem is as tall as the diameter of the bowl plus its height, and half again. The leaves usually need to be stripped from the stem.

2

3 Try to make the flowers look towards the centre of the arrangement and at each other. When subsidiary stems are used with the three main stems, these should always be shorter than the third stem. Points of iris leaves should turn inwards. Place leaves carefully between points of holder to hide them.

3

Sun Prayer

A curving stem of setsuka willow with Helichrysum petiolatum *and pansies, can be repeated in spring with narcissi*

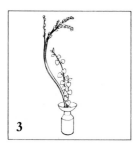

1 Cut a piece of living twig to wedge in the neck of the vase and place it in the best position for keeping the willow stem upright. The base of this stem must touch the bottom or side of the container or it will not stand well. A very narrow container may not need a twig.

2 Arrange the willow stem so that its curve is over, not beyond, the container. See that its proportions are right. It needs to be as long as the height of the container plus the diameter, and half this sum again. It can be more but should never be less.

3 The stems of *Helichrysum petiolatum* follow the willow's curve. Their soft downy texture contrasts prettily with the smooth brown bark of the willow and, later, with the velvety pansies. The second stem should be three-quarters the length of the willow. The third stem should be three-quarters the length of the second stem.

Geisha

Colourful nasturtiums and chlorophytum leaves – a pattern for all flowers with soft curving stems

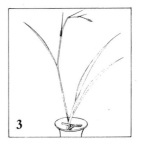

1 A forked twig is firmly in the mouth of the vase to support the stems. Cypress is a good wood for this purpose but any living twig that does not split easily will do. Cut the twig down the centre and wedge open the two arms with a small portion of twig.

2 Stems are supported against one of the arms of the forked twig or held in one angle or another according to their position. Try to get the tip of the tallest stem over the centre of the base of the container.

3 Two other pieces of chlorophytum form the important trio of tall stems. These should be arranged in the same portion of the forked twig as the tallest stem. Sometimes it is best to tie the three together with the tie, low down well below rim level. Arrange a few nasturtium flowers and some foliage to the lower part of the arrangement.

47

Summer Day

Cornflowers and a bleached twig, a pattern for all the daisy family

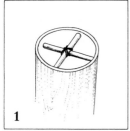

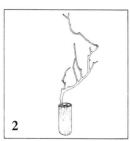

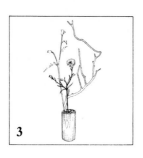

1 A good stem holder is easily made from crossed portions of green or living twigs bound together at the centre. Measure carefully so that they sit firmly in the mouth of the container and make sure that they will not move during arrangement or under pressure from stems.

2 The bleached branch of driftwood, found on the beach, rests in the angle of one of the quarters of the crossed twig. The base of its stem rests firmly on the floor of the container on the side opposite the point where the stem rises from the rim.

3 A slender stem with dainty leaves and buds is the second important stem. This is balanced by the tallest cornflower which rests against the bleached stem and rises from the same quarter of the holder. The trio is now complete. No other stems must be as long or longer than these.

Study in Form

Summer roses with preserved stems of alder catkins. Catkins and blossom with hothouse roses could be substituted in spring

1 The pinholder need not be large but it must be firm. A heavy stone will hide and anchor it later. Plasticine pills can be used as washers to hold the pinholder in place. Press them lightly on the dry base of the holder and then firmly press it home on the floor of the container.

2 Cut the base of the alder stem on a slant so it can be impaled easily. Let the tip of the tall alder stem lean away from the centre. Prune away side stems to make a definite but uncluttered silhouette. Keep the lower portion of the stem fairly free of side growths.

3 The second stem needs to be three-quarters the length of the tallest. Try to keep the stem end uncluttered and let it rise in line with the lower stem of the first. To make it lean properly, lay the stem base slightly horizontally, instead of vertically, on the pinpoints of the holder. Position the roses at the base of the design and cover the pinholder with an attractive stone.

Sparkle

Spray 'spider' chrysanthemums with driftwood show a pattern which can be used throughout the year

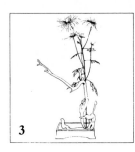

1 The three important stems in this arrangement are the tallest spray chrysanthemum, the tallest piece of driftwood and the short-stemmed chrysanthemums. The base of the driftwood is tapered to make arrangement easier. A bare branch or one with buds just opening, such as horse chestnut, can be used as an alternative to the driftwood.

2 The lower piece of driftwood is used mainly to hide the pinholder. It is placed in position early so that it can be firmly fixed in place. Subsequent stems are placed behind it. Its rough texture contrasts well with the ethereal flowers.

3 Spray chrysanthemums, grown all the year round nowadays, have long graceful stems and this arrangement is designed to make the most of this feature. Usually the sprays are a little too full for Japanese designs and will need to have some blooms or buds pruned away.

Orchid Dream

*Orchids are long lasting.
Cymbidiums arranged
with setsuka willow,
sansevieria and begonia
foliage*

1 This willow curves naturally but ordinary willow can be shaped by tying it in circles and soaking all night in a bowl of water. Alternatively, use driftwood or a slender house plant leaf such as a tall epiphyllum. Place the pinholder to one side of the dish.

2 The orchid spray is roughly three-quarters the length of the setsuka willow stem. Try to arrange the former so that each flower is prettily displayed: gauge which way blooms naturally face by turning the stem in the hand before impaling it on the pinholder.

3 The sansevieria leaf is three-quarters the length of the orchid stem. It leans with the willow although it cannot follow its curve. The lower part of the stem should be arranged so it cups round the orchid stem if possible, but the stones positioned later will mask it if this is not possible.

Follow a Line

Sometimes the very magnificence of the flowers to be arranged can be forbidding, especially when these have been grown to perfection. How is it possible, you wonder, to arrange them so that they fit aptly and attractively into your own surroundings? This can often be the case when flowers come as gifts or if they have to be bought, yet even flowers like these can be endowed with a softer grace by employing quite simple methods. All one needs to create a pleasing arrangement is to find a line to follow.

Actually, few stems are absolutely straight. More often one can detect a slight tendency to lean in one direction or another. This suggests the line to follow. Encourage all the flowers to go the same way so that they emphasise this angle no matter how slight. Sometimes it is possible to spotlight it further by pruning away some of the growth from one side of a stem.

For those who like to experiment, daffodils are both fun and stimulating to arrange and variations on their arrangement can be limitless. For instance, arrange the tallest stem at a slight angle and you quickly establish a line to follow as some illustrations in this chapter demonstrate.

Another simple method is to arrange uniform flowers in a curve, the blooms quite close but not hiding each other, thus presenting a thick line of colour. There are many other uniform flowers that can be treated this way, just as there are many variations that can be played on this theme. The arrangement 'Spring Pastels' (page 59) gives an example of tulips treated in this manner, the curve being extended here to make a long, lazy 'S'. From a close set curve, it is but a short step to arranging flowers so that they have more space between them and from there to filling the spaces between them with other contrasting materials. Often these can follow their own line so that you create a pattern within a pattern.

While one might find formal subjects to be challenging, informal materials and those with curving stems can be a great stimulus to the creative arranger. These suggest styles or presentations which are well worth exploring and which often result in exciting shapes and pleasing ensembles.

Besides being used on their own account, curving stems can be arranged with formal subjects. It is usually best to arrange the curving stems first and then to arrange the others within their limits, although not necessarily so strictly as the Japanese rules dictate.

Curving stems of moluccella flow from a triangular group of roses and hypericum berries

Golden Medley

One bunch of daffodils can make an important decoration if the flowers are supplemented with foliage and blossom

1 Metal containers bring extra life and colour to flower arrangements in winter. Also, the flowers last longer in them because metal delays bacterial activity and so keeps the water fresher. The vase is filled with wire-netting. A tall stem of cornus is arranged first from which the lower side stems have been pruned away.

2 Green conifer and golden cupressus furnish the bare lower stems of the cornus and link the sparse branches with the showy flowers. These are bought in bud, to last longer and to be enjoyed as they open. Be sure to insert daffodils through the mesh, otherwise it may slice the stems up their centres.

3 To follow the curve of the design, all the flowers face the same way. The tallest stem has its base only just inside the container and is pinned in position with a cut end of wire-netting. Be careful to top up water level daily.

High Elegance

Lovely, forced bulbous irises with trimmings from the house plant rhoicissus, in a queen conch shell

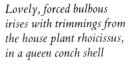

1 Shells make lovely containers for spring flowers. First handle the shell to determine how it best stands firm and to ensure that it will take water without spilling. Place well-soaked foamed plastic inside the shell to ensure continual moisture, and press wire-netting into the shell mouth.

2 Irises, the fleurs-de-lys of the ancient banners, look loveliest in silhouette. In this arrangement provision has been made for each flower to be well displayed. Start with the tallest stem and work to the base, shortening each stem so that each flower is just below the one above.

3 Irises are best bought or picked as buds which are less likely to be damaged in transport. When arranging them, allow for petal expansion. Place the first two stems almost vertically, but lean the rest so that they appear to flow out from the base of the tallest one. Finally position the trails of rhoicissus.

Shell Patterns

Dolphin-shaped vases in metals or ceramics are great favourites with flower arrangers, mainly I suspect, because the fish-shaped pedestal which holds aloft a shell-shaped bowl suggests a graceful line for them to follow.

Curves like those of the dolphin's body prompt the arranger to follow free, wide-ranging lines. If you have a garden look for those parts of a plant which have been sculpted or shaped by the wind or some other cause and use them to provide interesting flowing shapes.

There are certain flower stems which once cut and stood in water lose their straight lines and become curved, even serpentine. Take note of any of these which behave this way and exploit this tendency when you arrange them. The pretty white-flowered dead nettle is an example and so is the closely related apple-green moluccella, which fortunately for those who have no gardens, can often be bought (it can also be dried).

The most helpful thing to do before beginning to assemble an arrangement is to handle the curving stems, getting to know their potential, arranging one here, perhaps upright and leaning to the left and another flowing from its base downwards to the right, until the pattern or the style best followed suddenly becomes apparent.

But as we have seen and will continue to discover, few aspects of flower arrangement can be strictly zoned, one naturally merges into another. In this arrangement the attractiveness of the line of the container and the curving stems and shapes it holds is further enhanced by the colour harmony of the flowers, leaves and fruits. The dark, seaweed green of the dolphin vase suggests that it should hold colours which were mostly in the same colour range. Even so, fancy took me a little further than colour itself, for it seemed so apt to follow the fish theme and associate moluccella's shell-studded stems and the pearly honesty and rose with the dolphin.

The 'shells' grow in whorls along the stems. Where these were shortened, the whorls were arranged separately on short stem lengths at the centre and low in the arrangement.

Select stems of moluccella which have curved well, and position them so they follow the line of the dolphin vase. Then push the maple leaves into the face of the foamed plastic at the front of the arrangement

A dolphin vase holds moluccella, honesty, maple leaves, hypericum berries and one pearly rose.

Glint of Spring

Daffodils, pussy willow,
Begonia rex and
variegated ivy leaves

1 Put a ball of wire-netting in the mouth of the jug. Hook two or three of the cut ends over the rim. Pull up some other ends to grip the stems. Insert the pussy willow and pull it until it leans attractively. Secure it in position with the wire ends. Prune side stems where these spoil the line.

2 Arrange some shorter willow stems at rim level. Use others to 'sketch' the outline of the arrangement. Place two large begonia leaves at the centre with the tips of each following the line of the willow. Use any other attractive leaf with harmonising hues if begonias are not available.

3 Buy daffodils in bud or only just opening. Select the tallest stem and place it high, pinning it in position with the wire ends if necessary. So long as an inch (2·5 cm) of the stem is in water the flowers will be all right. Arrange the other flowers and buds to follow the line of the willow and leaves.

58

Spring Pastels

Tulips with young maple leaves and blossom

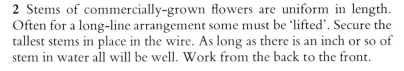

1 In this arrangement each flower is displayed to advantage, and at the same time, it has space to grow and expand. Stems need to be held securely. The vase has a narrow mouth but even so wire-netting should be used to hold them. This should fill the container from base to rim.

2 Stems of commercially-grown flowers are uniform in length. Often for a long-line arrangement some must be 'lifted'. Secure the tallest stems in place in the wire. As long as there is an inch or so of stem in water all will be well. Work from the back to the front.

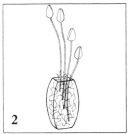

3 The tulip below the rim level can be arranged this way: gently hold the flower in place, pass wire-netting ends round the stem, press on these to push the stem down to continue the line. Some leaves should be stripped from the tulips or the arrangement will be too dense. Then arrange the maple stems in line with tulips.

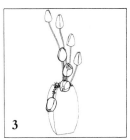

Blossom Time

White lilac and rhododendrons in a white pedestal vase

1 Lilac or syringa lasts much longer in water if all the foliage is removed. After this, split the stem ends and stand them in boiling water until the blossoms are firm and turgid. They can then be arranged in shallower water on a pinholder covered with large mesh wire-netting as shown.

2 Place the tallest stem in position first. If it seems to be top-heavy because of the weight of blossom, carefully snip away one or more pieces of blossom and either arrange these lower down or use them in some other decoration. Be sure to split the ends of all re-cut stems upwards for an inch or less according to their length.

3 Rhododendrons also need to have some foliage removed, merely to lessen the density of their effect. These flowers open well in water so they can be picked in bud. Remove some foliage from near the flowers, but the leaves on the lower part of the stem help to wedge the sprays in place.

Summer Spray

Sweet peas and pansies in a quickly assembled arrangement, held by a little dolphin vase

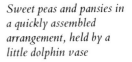

1 Sweet peas grow daily once the plants begin blooming, so it is useful to have a quick method for their arrangement! These flowers last best in shallow water. The stiff stems are easily inserted into foamed plastic but the soft-stemmed pansies are easier arranged in wire-netting.

2 Flowers, when perched as gracefully on their stems as are sweet peas, look best if they are fairly informally arranged. Their curves suit the style of the dolphin container and the flower shapes are shown to advantage. The foamed plastic will hold them in just the position you want.

3 As they are being arranged, sweet pea stems should be cut on a slant. This not only ensures that they go into the stem holder easily but also that they take up water rapidly. Once they are allowed to wilt, they never look so fresh and colourful again.

Using Colour

It is probably the colour of flowers that attracts us to them in our early years. Consider, for instance, how children love buttercups and dandelions and their excitement at the sight of a mass of field poppies. Later we come to love them for their individuality; daisies, primroses and pansies, for example, are so easy to recognise, presenting as they do such endearing faces. Later still we go on to appreciate their varied forms and textures, but even so, for some it is always floral colour which has the greatest appeal, witness the aim of so many gardeners to create a riot of colour in their garden borders.

One of the most exciting things that flower arrangement has to offer is the opportunity to 'paint' living pictures from glorious colours and to create exciting harmonies. This is open as much to those who have no gardens as to those who can gather unlimited material.

For many of us the first consideration always is to use those flowers which are at hand or which are cheap and plentiful. The season does not always follow the demands of the flower arranger and often mixtures have to be fortuitous rather than planned on a long-term basis.

In the home where flower arrangement plays an important decorative role, colour is of great importance. In modern homes where no fireplace exists or where no fire is lit, a warm flower arrangement can make all the

A copper goblet holds flowers, foliage and berries of nearly related colours

difference to the atmosphere of a room. Besides being attractive it can offer a comforting focal point, a feature sadly missing from many rooms. A full arrangement at the centre of the dining table serves the same purpose and has the quality of uniting the company assembled around the table. Here the colours of the flowers can be harmonised with china, linen and candles. In summer flower arrangements of white, cream, pale yellow, green and blue harmonies present a cool aspect.

Plain coloured walls offer guidance on the colours of the flowers to be placed against them. Where the walls are covered with a pattern, flowers of similar colours and hues can be used. In this case it may prove best to group the floral colours in larger masses than are used in the pattern. Alternatively, and this is usually the more successful method, select just one colour at a time from the pattern and base the arrangement on this. Obviously containers should also suit the setting.

Naturally, each arranger will be drawn towards the colours which he or she finds most pleasing. These are bound to differ from person to person and some will find soft colour harmonies most pleasing while others prefer to be stimulated by vivid colour contrasts. There do exist a few guidelines which the inexperienced may find helpful.

Basically we turn to the rainbow. Here a sequence of colours occurs quite naturally and is unchanging. One sees red, orange, yellow, green, blue and purple, always in that order.

There exist three primary colours, red,

yellow and blue. These overlap at their edges, one with the other, to create secondary colours, orange, green and purple. The centre zone of each colour, primary and secondary, is true and really intense. From this point though, and on each side, it changes as it moves towards the neighbouring colours, taking on first just a little of their colour as it draws nearer until it changes completely. This way we see a colour which is more red than orange yet not quite true red, or a green which definitely shows that it contains blue, or a purple which veers towards red, and so on through the entire spectrum. We give these nuances of colour familiar names, usually of familiar objects and speak of them for instance as salmon pink, apricot yellow, cherry red or cerise, lavender and emerald green. Technically these are all hues of one colour or another.

Many people prefer the hues to the true colours. Certainly soft, pleasing arrangements can be made from flowers in certain hues. However, those made from flowers of full colours are often essential because so many of our more plentiful flowers fall into this category. They can be highly decorative, especially when arrangements are to be made for important occasions, or when it is essential that they shall be noticed immediately.

The term 'pastel shades' is often used to describe pale colours or hues, but this is really a contradictory term because a shade is really a colour or hue that has a shadow in it, that is to say, contains grey or black. On the other hand a tint is a hue or colour that has light or white in it.

The flower arranger will find it helpful to understand that the colours in the spectrum are related in two ways. For reasons of clarity when discussing colour and colour harmony we convert the rainbow colour band into a wheel, so that we see the two ends joined with red next to the purple. Once we have made a colour wheel it can be seen that there are opposite colours. These are complementary to each other. Thus we oppose red to green, orange to blue and purple to yellow. This follows a natural law. To prove it you can

draw a red circle on a piece of white paper, gaze at it for a minute or two and then turn your eyes quickly to another piece of blank white paper or to a plain white wall. A green spot of the same size will appear. This means that the brain has compensated the red-tired eyes. It will react in the same way to the other colours, presenting the complementary colour on each occasion.

Some flowers are made of complementary colours and it is both entertaining and helpful to study the colour harmonies of individual flowers. The handsome strelitzia is a fine example of complementary colour harmony. However, more flowers show a different colour harmony. These are in related or analagous colours, which are simply neighbouring colours, near to each other in the spectrum, easily appreciated by studying the colour wheel. Several of the arrangements in this chapter are based on this natural colour harmony.

We have seen that when two primary colours are mixed secondary colours are created. What happens when two complementary colours are mixed? We find that 'broken' colours are created. Red and green make a warm brown, blue and orange a pleasant grey, purple and yellow a tan. As you would expect, complementary hues present variations on these broken colours. An arranger who wishes further to explore this fascinating subject is advised to experiment with a few water colour paints. These reveal all kinds of unsuspected liaisons.

To know even a little about broken colours does have a practical purpose. For example, the knowledge offers you a guide to what colours to choose for containers for certain arrangements if these are not to match exactly the colour of the flowers or perhaps just one of the components in the flower mixture. It is reassuring to know that you can select a container with confidence, knowing that all will be in harmony, if that is your intention.

Apart from finding the broken colour, your choice for the colour of the container can also be suggested by the flowers themselves, and not necessarily the whole flower but just some part of it. For instance, in the arrangement 'Pedestal Grace' (page 67) you can see how the colour of the glass container matches the centres of the little pompon chrysanthemums. This is the only match between flower and container. The harmony of the arrangement goes further. The same little centres and the undersides of the petals also carry a touch of a purple, only noticeable on close study. This colour is picked up again by the ornamental kale and is seen as a tint in the pink chicory.

The container is often partly hidden by the flowers, but even so it should be in harmony with them. White, black, brown and 'natural' hues are all fairly safe when used with almost every flower. Metal containers can be roughly grouped into orange copper, yellow brass and white silver. Pewter is splendidly neutral. Where no problem exists about the quantity of flowers available, it is a pleasant exercise to begin with a container and then to search for harmonising materials to furnish it.

Some of the loveliest arrangements, and possibly the most popular among skilled flower arrangers, are those which are composed of hues, tints, shades and tones of green. There are examples of such arrangements in other chapters (defined later). Besides being decorative and extraordinarily restful when set about a home, these are also 'safe' because green harmonises with every other colour.

Just as safe are monochromatic arrangements of white flowers or those with a small amount of green showing among the white flowers. This is intentional. It is possible by defoliating all leafy stems to eliminate most of this colour. There are some arrangers who take even greater licence and remove other parts of flowers so as to keep strictly within the colour zone. Fortunately, many flowers have smooth stems and offer no problems of an abundance of green. So far as the others are concerned, surely the characters of the flowers we use are as important as their colours. Often when we remove all their leaves we take away an important feature of their individuality. It is always possible to arrange the flowers so that the main colour dominates.

House Warming

Orange and white carnations with roses, double tulips and eucalyptus buds in tiered bowls

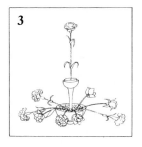

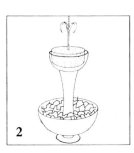

1 Tall flower arrangements can be built up by making tiers from two or more bowls supported on wine glasses, candlesticks or narrow vases. Two brass bowls are used here, the smaller one is supported in the rim of a tall metal vase.

2 Fill the top bowl with a block of foamed plastic and fix a ring of large mesh wire-netting round the base of the supporting vase in the lower bowl. Place the top flower in position first. Fairly short-stemmed flowers can be used in a tall arrangement of this kind.

3 Arrange side stems in the bottom tier: if a wide cone is wanted, bring these out far beyond the side stems of the tier above. For a more compact shape, keep these stems roughly equal in span with those above. All the flowers should appear to flow from a central point.

Pedestal Grace

Pink- and blue-studded chicory stems with pompon chrysanthemums, ornamental kale and pineapple mint leaves in a glass pedestal bowl

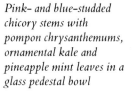

1 Any kind of pedestal adds grace to short-stemmed flowers. This glass dish is too shallow to hold enough water for fresh flowers so another dish has been fixed to it. Plasticine pills and adhesive clay can be used for this purpose quite effectively.

2 A large pinholder is fixed to the base of the dish in the same way. It is absolutely essential that all surfaces should be dry, otherwise the 'washers' will not hold firm. It is always wise to secure pinholders in this way because then the arrangement can be moved safely when required.

3 The tall stems of chicory are arranged first. Only the tallest one is vertical. All the others lean away from it in one direction or another. The first stems should go well back to leave room for a mass of flowers. Once the background is made the kale leaves, chrysanthemums and mint are set in place.

67

Summer Medley

Easily-grown annuals –
malope, poppy, candytuft,
cornflowers, marigolds
and nigella among them –
in a traditional pattern

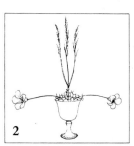

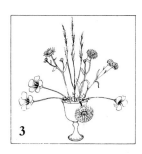

1 The stem ends must be stripped of all foliage or this will decay under the water. This means also that stems are left smooth and thin and will go easily through wire-netting. Place this with cut ends uppermost and, if stems are very fine, pull the netting up at the back.

2 The malope blooms on each side of the arrangement, defining its width, are laterals. So far as many plants are concerned, these are often best for furnishing a vase, and, by leaving the main stems growing the garden is not robbed. Tall spikes are from orach (atriplex or mountain spinach) with burgundy-coloured foliage and stems.

3 Sketch in the outline. Remember that flowers look more effective if small groups are formed, rather as they grow in the border, than if they are mixed in an all-over pattern. Poppies should be gathered just as the buds are about to break and their stem ends should be singed to seal them.

Autumn Harmony

Delphiniums, nerines, Michaelmas daisies and hydrangeas in a tall glass

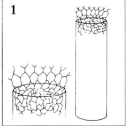

1 Stems seen through glass should look smooth and neat, so carefully strip the base of each one. Do not fill the entire container with wire-netting as this will be unsightly, simply push it in the top portion only, allowing a good piece to remain above rim level.

2 Pull up and fan out the netting at the back to make a support for the tall subjects. The stems can then lean against the wire, after their bases are passed down through the shallow layer of netting. The cut ends of wire can also be used to 'pin' a stem in the required position.

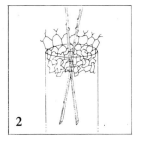

3 Make an outline of the shape of the arrangement with the tall stems at the back. Side branches cut from main stems of Michaelmas daisies do admirably at the lower levels. Arrange some of these to flow forward. Once the background is made, fill in with the rounded shapes in the foreground. Snip off any faded daisies daily.

Pendent Patterns

When the aim of the flower arranger is to present colour, it seems only natural that the flowers are most often assembled in full, massed arrangements. Those illustrated in this chapter mostly follow the traditional styles, although some present variations on the old themes. In each case the colour of the container is part of the general harmony.

However, it is not essential that the old styles should be followed. So much depends upon the material which is to be arranged. For instance, in early spring often there are not the same round, robust flowers which are available in summer, nor are there so many of them. Arrangements therefore have to be designed to suit whatever is in season.

It is possible not only to establish a flowing line but also to provide a good area of colour by using branches of blossom, flowering currant in this case. By carefully spacing the branches and by discerning how best the flowers should be displayed, these can be made to occupy a fair amount of space. In the arrangement illustrated the laterals cut from the portion of stem which goes inside the container have been carefully saved and arranged to hang prettily pendent over the rim of the container, thus adding to the general shape of the arrangement and to the amount of colour.

Within this framework quite small flowers have been arranged. Two principles of mine have been followed. One is that where flowers have a particularly engaging or sculpted form, this should be exploited. Therefore, some of the little muscari (in form like little bunches of grapes, hence their popular name of grape hyacinth) have been lifted from the mass and are well featured. The other principle is that where small flowers which also have short stems are to be used, they can be posied or otherwise massed together so as to occupy the space of a single large flower. The daisies demonstrate how this works.

The colour harmony is based on nearly related colours. The container is white, like some of the daisies' petals. The rose colour of their centres and tips matches the currant blossom. This rose is really a hue of purple. So with the muscari blue and the leaf green an analogous colour harmony is created.

Make the outline of the design with the flowering-currant stems so that all the flower racemes fall in the same direction. Push the base of the tallest stem deep enough down through the netting into the foamed plastic for it to hold fast. Then fan out the grape hyacinths to the left. Arrange the daisies at the centre last of all

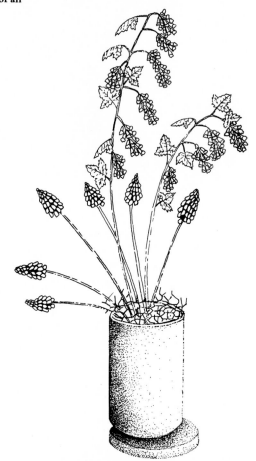

Early-flowering currant with double daisies and grape hyacinths.

Ruby Riches

Dahlias, chrysanthemums and annual carnations with nigella in a lustre urn

1 Cut a piece of large mesh wire-netting measuring twice the widest diameter of the vase and twice its depth. Push it into a U shape and place it in the vase. Hook netting ends round the handle at each end. Netting in highly glazed containers tends to slip and this secures it.

2 Arrange the tallest stems, securing them with netting should this be necessary. Let the side stems flow at right angles or more to the centre. Heavy blooms are given a little more support if they rest on the rim, but these also can be held fast by the little snag ends of wire (see drawing 3).

3 When mixed flowers resemble each other in shape, an arrangement is more effective if the stems are cut at greatly varying lengths so that some of the blooms can be recessed. Clusters, such as chrysanthemums, can be divided so that one gets a long-stemmed flower and one or more short-stemmed blooms.

Harmony

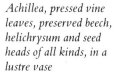

Achillea, pressed vine leaves, preserved beech, helichrysum and seed heads of all kinds, in a lustre vase

1 Dried materials are light in weight, and even a large arrangement can be easily knocked over unless precautions are taken. Where possible, use heavy containers. Alternatively, weight them by pouring in sand or gravel to at least one third of the depth. Stem holders, such as wire-netting, can then be placed on top.

2 Collect or grow tall tapering materials for the edges of arrangements which contain heavy flowers like these flat golden achillea. Defining the height and shape are plantain (a weed), and seed stems and barley, both of which are best gathered green. Brown rushes should be cut young.

3 After defining the dimensions, sketch in the outline of the arrangement. Grade the materials as they are arranged so that as work proceeds from the edges into the centre, the main materials become denser and larger. Pressed leaves may need false stems so stick straws to their backs with adhesive tape or Copydex.

Distinctive Containers

If you adopt a liberal attitude about what 'vases' you are prepared to use you need never be at a loss to create unusual arrangements. So many of the objects about the house, never intended originally to hold flowers, will in fact often prove to be ideal for this purpose. Besides these, there are numerous objects worth collecting, sometimes for a few pence, for future use. Anything which takes your eye and fancy and kept in store will one day be seen as just the very thing you need.

Naturally those vessels which are watertight are likely to prove to be the most useful. Incidentally, look for these in the kitchen as well as the drawing room. Many oven dishes have distinctive lines and pleasing textures which enhance certain flowers.

If there is danger of moisture escaping, containers can be lined with a double thickness of kitchen foil or plastic film, in which case it is best to use a foamed plastic stem holder rather than wire netting which might pierce the lining.

For dried flower arrangements where no water is involved, the choice is even wider. Heavy objects are useful because dried materials are light in weight. Those of metal such as copper and brass also provide a warm glow which brings life to preserved and pressed materials. However, wooden objects also harmonise with all perpetuelles beautifully. Where necessary containers can be weighted with sand, gravel or some other heavy substance and the stem holder placed on this, as we show in one of the arrangements illustrated here.

Candlesticks can be fitted with candle cups or small bowls. Statuettes can be made to hold a supplementary vessel for water and stem holder. Thus these ornaments are converted into pedestal vases.

It is sometimes helpful to use more than one container, one inside another, as we saw in the last chapter in the arrangement 'House Warming' (page 66), or if you wish to lift or isolate one kind of flower or some other component, as you can see here in the arrangement made in a shallow basket.

Flowers suit old pitchers of pottery or metal as well as other kinds of jugs and tankards. These can be turned in such a way that their handles are hidden and they present a vase shape, but this is to subdue the character of the vessel. Keep the handle on show as an important part of the ensemble. Most times it establishes a line for you to follow. It will certainly add distinction to the arrangement and lift it from the usual patterns.

A distinctively patterned wine jug holds an unusual winter arrangement of fatsia leaves and flowers and ivy

Snowdrift

Chincherinchees, contrasted with dark green glossy box leaves, in a pattern which can be copied for most flowers

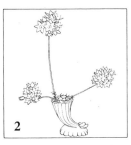

1 When a container has a curve like this cornucopia, the flowers look more graceful if they can be arranged to follow its line. To do this, arrange the tallest stem first, well back against the rim of the container. Grip the stem with the wire-netting ends.

2 To accentuate the curve gently press on the wire round the stem until the latter falls into the required position. Try to make all subsequent stems appear as though they spring from the base of the tallest 'guide' stem. Arrange the first sideward pointing stems to define the shape and scope of the design.

3 Chincherinchees, like most other bulb flowers, do not require deep water, so these intermediate stems need not reach right down into the vase. The wire-netting, through which the stems are inserted, will hold them firmly. Sprays of box can be cut to make attractive, low-curving lines.

Spring Gift

Scillas, snowdrops, crocuses and daffodils with budding twigs, heather, kale leaves, ivy and primroses

1 If the basket is not already tin-lined, line it with thick or double plastic, black polythene for preference, or cooking foil. Choose small pinholders for the tall twigs and wedge these in place using foamed plastic and/or stones or small pieces of wire-netting. Alternatively, use small containers, such as cream or yoghurt cartons, to hold separate groups.

2 The cartons can be made shorter and bowl-shaped by pouring boiling water into them. Fill the cartons with stem holders such as wire netting or foamed plastic. Wedge them in place by filling the intervening spaces with more stem holders to hold small bunches, individual stems or entire roots.

3 Have some moss ready to wedge flowers growing from bulbs or corms, such as crocuses, so that they stand upright. If you use the moss to hide the containers, see that none of it hangs over the rim of the basket to act as a siphon. Leaves and snippets of evergreen can also be used to hide the containers.

Garden Fragrance

Roses and lavender in a Prinknash pottery mug

1 Place a piece of foamed plastic at the bottom of the mug to hold the stem ends of the lavender. Fill the rest of the mug with large mesh wire-netting, hooking two cut ends round the top of the handle to anchor the netting firmly.

2 Arrange the tall stems of lavender, placing each one down through the netting into the foam. Each stem is slightly curved, so turn them so that they appear to be flowing away from the handle. Separate them a little but keep fairly close to give the appearance of a sheaf.

3 The roses should now be arranged. Those with tall, straight stems can be taken right down into the foam, but others should be arranged at any level according to their size. Keep some foliage on the upper part of the rose stems unless this is likely to hide the blooms in which case it can be removed and the leaves arranged individually lower down.

Flame Holder

Snapdragons, begonias, nasturtiums and annual chrysanthemums in a candlestick holder

1 Candlesticks make delightful pedestals for flower arrangements, especially for tables or sideboards when a pair can be used. Candlecups can be bought from flower shops, and some of these are complete with a ring-shaped pinholder which also allows a space for the candle. Alternatively, use a normal pinholder fixed firmly in place, or a cylinder of well-soaked foamed plastic.

2 When stems of varying thicknesses are to be arranged, impale a ball of large mesh wire-netting on the pinholder. If the arrangement is to stand in the centre of the table, the tallest stem should be arranged in the middle of the holder. This should be the only upright stem.

3 Arrange side stems to flow at a low level so that the flower holder is completely hidden. To aid arrangement, set aside flowers with curved stems, or pendant blooms which fall naturally, and arrange these at rim level and lower down. Hook a little piece of cut wire-netting round the stem if the flower seems insecure.

Engagement Party

Carole roses, Limonium suworowii *(statice) and Dusty Miller (senecio) leaves*

1 If flowers have to be moved around, it is best to use a block of foamed plastic which will not spill and will hold the stems quite fast. This can be cut to fit any vase or bowl and should be moistened daily for as long as the flowers last.

2 Choose the tallest stemmed rose and place it as far back against the rim as possible. Arrange a tuft of the senecio (or any other soft and pretty foliage) at its base. Put another rose just above rim level to flow outwards.

3 Let the roses flow out from behind the leaves, but first arrange the tallest stems. If these have branches, leave one rose and cut off the others to arrange lower down. Later, fill in space with individual leaves and tall stems of statice or something of similar shape and texture.

Pompon

Giant onion, or allium, flowers are simply arranged with driftwood. Use this pattern for all flowers with leafless stems

1 As we are following an oriental style here, the tallest stem needs to be at least one-and-a-half times as tall as the width of the container plus the height but it can be a great deal taller. Much of the beauty of alliums lies in the long stems supporting the handsome globular blooms, and this has been featured in this design.

2 The second stem is roughly three-quarters the length of the tallest, and the shortest stem is three-quarters the length of the second stem. All are held safely on the pinholder. Each stem should lean a little away from the other.

3 Before arrangement, three or four pills of plasticine or adhesive clay should be pressed to the dry base of the holder which in turn is pressed on to the dry base of the container. The driftwood in the bowl will hide the pinholder and that round the base will mask the container.

81

Sea Harvest

*Flowers and shells go
beautifully together;
acrocliniums, statice,
honesty and hydrangeas
capture the soft hues of
mother-of-pearl*

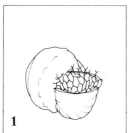

1 First find how the shell stands best. Study the aperture and decide how the flowers should flow from it. Almost fill it with dry foamed plastic and insert a piece of large mesh wire-netting in the mouth of the shell. Use the cut ends of wire to hook round the shell rim if necessary.

2 As dried flower stems do not need to reach water, their arrangement really presents no problem. The acroclinium goes down vertically into the wire-netting but not far inside the shell. Hold it just where required, either by pinching the wire against its stem or by hooking a wire end round it.

3 Stems on the horizontal can be arranged the same way and some of the statice group are held in a similar manner. Then, when the other materials are introduced, their stems can be inserted from the front right into the heart of the shell. The stems gradually interlock and hold each other firm.

Treen Collection

Grevillea, eucalyptus, bracken, beech leaves and mast, honesty, pussy willow and cones

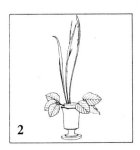

1 Weight the vase by pouring in sand to a third of the depth. Top up with a piece of foamed plastic allowing this to protrude a little. Mount the cones and beech leaf clusters, retain an inch or so of the main stem. Mount the individual fern fronds in fans of five.

2 Strip the dyed grevillea stem to give a tapering shape. Save stripped leaves to use individually at the back of the arrangement as required. Place beech clusters round the side, pointing slightly downwards. Their short stem ends can be pushed horizontally into the side of the protruding foam.

3 Begin filling in towards the central area. Small twigs of pussy willow can be lengthened by inserting florists' wire in the stem base. Alternatively it can be twisted round the stems. Work from the back to the rim displaying each component but slanting each stem from the centre until the lower subjects are at rim level.

83

Individual Flowers

Flowers bought from store, shop, stall or nursery are most likely to be mass produced. This means that they will probably be uniform, of equal size and height. This may not be pleasing to the flower arranger who has discovered the disadvantages of perfection, but there is one great thing in favour of these commercially-produced beauties. So much thought, time and care has been lavished upon them that so long as they were newly marketed when bought they should last well. Time and trouble taken over their early arrangement is well rewarded because except for topping up the water level, they should remain looking lovely for days.

One drawback when certain flowers last a long time in water is that their leaves do not always have the same stamina. These may fade after a few days and become unattractive. Chrysanthemums are an example. Such flowers can be arranged with plenty of other kinds of foliage in the first place so that when the fading leaves are removed they are not really missed. Alternatively, the flowers can be stripped while still in situ and then provided with leaves of a different kind, using these to mask the stripped stems. Or the arrangement can be dissembled, the flower stems stripped and a new arrangement designed with new supporting materials. One way to deal with this is to mix younger flowers with the old, the new foliage on the

Golden Chain – *prettily pendent laburnum blossom in a low brown dish whose interior harmonises with the flowers' colour*

one helping to mask the barren stems of the other. Incidentally, it is sometimes worth saving any kind of good foliage left over from a previous arrangement to help furnish a later one. Some well-shaped calyces left empty after faded petals have been plucked out can also be decorative and useful.

Where a mass of colour is more important than style, vases can be kept well filled by mixing old and new. Try it with daffodils and their buds, anemones and roses. So long as containers are scrupulously clean it should be necessary only to top up the water level daily.

Where flowers are stiff-stemmed and few in number they can effectively be arranged in curves, lazy-S lines or simple triangular patterns, even when only three blooms are to be used. If their stems are leafless you can use fruits, even certain kinds of vegetables, individual leaves and branches or trails of other kinds of foliage to help smudge the too-formal outlines of the blooms and also to provide contrasting form, texture and extra colour, or should this be required, bulk.

Arrangers who have no garden sometimes find it difficult to locate a supply or source of diverse foliage. For this purpose a stock of easy-to-grow-and-care-for house plants such as ivy, rhoicissus and the tradescantias from which trails can be cut, and *Begonia rex* and others from which individual leaves can be taken, will prove invaluable. A little light trimming does well-grown plants no harm. After arrangement most of the stems and leaves can be rooted as cuttings to provide new plants and so increase the stock.

Winter Cheer

Anemone coronaria *or*
poppy anemones

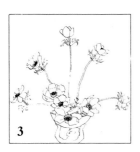

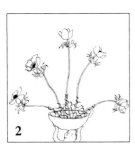

1 Give anemones a long drink in tepid water, about 21°C (70°F) before arranging them in fairly shallow containers. Top up the water level daily. Use large mesh wire-netting pulled high in the centre to support the tallest stems. Hook ends over the rim to anchor the mesh.

2 Select the tallest stems from two or more bunches and arrange these first. Anemone stems tend to grow and curve after arrangement so merely cut stems at varying levels and do not expect their positions to remain static. Hold side stems in low positions by hooking wire ends round them near rim level.

3 Buy young flowers with the pollen still unspilled on the bases of their petals. Some will mature before others and as they fade replace with a new bunch at a time. Thus you are constantly bringing young flowers into the arrangement. As the fresh flowers are arranged, recess some stems at rim level to hide the stem holder.

Scented Rainbow

Freesias with ivy trails and snippets of cupressus and peperomia

1 Unlike most flowers that grow from bulbs or corms, freesias enjoy plenty of water and humidity so a deep container is advisable. Half fill it with foamed plastic and top this with wire-netting. Keep cut ends of netting uppermost so that these can be used to support slender stems.

2 Make a foundation of various types of foliage. Mass short-stemmed pieces fairly low to give body to the arrangement because freesia stems are very frail and bunches are usually leafless. Group the largest leaves in or near the centre and put the tapering trails at the edges.

3 Define the shape of the arrangement with the longest stems. Experiment with the flowers to find which way they tend to fall and arrange them to flow in this direction. Group the colours to get their full value but do not make this too obvious. White at the centre of the arrangement will accentuate the hues which surround it.

Harvest of Roses

Floribunda roses in a classical arrangement which could be used on a small scale for the home or, on a larger one, for a wedding

1 Although the rose stems are fairly uniform in length, some have been heightened artificially. Wire-netting, cut longer than the required length of twice the height of the container, is pulled up in the centre so that it can securely hold an empty tablet tube.

2 No stem holders are necessary in a narrow tablet tube. First gauge and cut the stems which are to go in it, and then use one to wedge the others in place. A leaf or two will also help hold the flowers in position.

3 The remaining roses are arranged beneath in the lower container so they hide the tube. When using supplementary containers in this way, always arrange them first so that they can be wedged and hidden before the other stems are positioned. More than one tube can be used for very large arrangements.

Spangles

Spider chrysanthemums

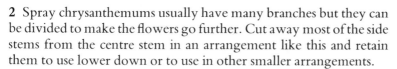

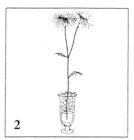

1 Year round, spray chrysanthemum grown by modern methods have lush, soft stems and delicate summery flowers, unlike the seasonal sturdy blooms of autumn. They like plenty of water and should have a long deep drink in tepid water before arrangement. Half fill a deep vase with foamed plastic and top this with some large mesh wire-netting.

2 Spray chrysanthemums usually have many branches but they can be divided to make the flowers go further. Cut away most of the side stems from the centre stem in an arrangement like this and retain them to use lower down or to use in other smaller arrangements.

3 Work from the centre outwards to left and right, shortening the stems as necessary, to make a symmetrical arrangement. Then work from the back to the rim leaning each stem a little further away from the centre towards the rim. Strip the leaves from the stem ends. Cut the ends on a slant as stems are shortened. Then recess the short-stemmed blooms.

Autumn Harvest

*Chrysanthemum blooms
last longer than their
leaves. Honesty 'moons',
barley and yellow kale
leaves fill the gaps*

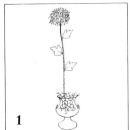

1 Chrysanthemums last best if they have plenty of water. It must be clean and be kept clean. Strip the leaves from the portion of stem to go under water and insert them through wire-netting for at least a quarter of the stem length.

2 If stems are of uniform length, when arranging, shorten each stem a little so that each flower shows to advantage. Use the cut ends of wire-netting, which should be arranged uppermost, to hold the flower at the required angle. The wider the mouth of the vase, the more spreading the arrangement can be.

3 Fill in the spaces between the flowers and arrange this supplementary material to give an attractive outline to the whole arrangement. Cut or pull up roots of honesty from the end of July onwards and before the frosts come. Hang them upside down to dry and become pale in a cool shed.

Tropical Magic

Long-lasting, brilliant anthuriums, or palette flowers, arranged with an assortment of house plant foliage and eucalyptus blossom

1 To fix pinholders really firmly so that they will not tilt if heavy stems are arranged on them or move if the arrangement is carried, place three or more small pills of plasticine or adhesive clay on the base of the pinholder. It is important that all surfaces are dry.

2 Press the pills lightly on the base of the pinholder and push this hard against the floor of the container. The pills will become flattened and should anchor the holder. Some stems need to be arranged vertically on the points. Others, like the leaf on the right, can be slanted across them.

3 Arrange each anthurium so that it shows to advantage. Some stems will have to be shortened or else one flower will hide another. Position the leaves and the eucalyptus to hide the pinholder, for this should never show in a finished arrangement. Sometimes attractive stones are used for this purpose.

Flowers
and Fruits

The decorative use of all kinds of fruits offers unlimited scope in creating exciting arrangements either made exclusively from them or with flowers and foliage. An everyday and most simple method is to use some of the edible kinds which would otherwise rest in a fruit dish, or perhaps in the kitchen, as a temporary boost to flowers. On the other hand, fruits found in the garden or hedgerow, under trees and on the common or moor can be used as a source of inspiration or to eke out precious or expensive blooms, or perhaps to provide contrasting or complementary colours, textures and form to an assortment of flowers and foliage. Exotic fruits, both dried and preserved, can be bought from florist shops and some garden centres and will last for years. These can be used with fresh or dried flowers.

Probably the most popular fruits are berries which are as diverse, beautiful and almost as versatile as the flowers themselves. Like the flowers, these will need careful conditioning (see page 11) before arrangement so that they take water well. They also need grooming so that damaged foliage and barren twigs are removed.

Naturally one thinks of fruits mainly in autumn, but they can be used the year round. Daffodils look lovely with branches of light brown larch cones, with oranges and lemons or with magenta-coloured stems of forced

China Pattern – *ornamental gourds and spray chrysanthemums match the colours in the pattern of the china, plate and bowl*

rhubarb with acid yellow coral-like, leafy tops. In summer there are many attractive unripe green fruits, grapes, currants, privet, elder to mention but a few, and clusters of green apples, pears and quinces which might be just the ingredient to give distinction to an all-green decoration.

Incidentally, most fruits and flowers get on well together, but ripe apples give off a gas which affects certain kinds of flowers and makes them 'sleepy' or closed-up and are best not used. However, ripe apples can be used safely with all kinds of foliage.

Most often fruits look best when they are arranged with their flower end central, but this need not be a hard and fast rule. Some stem ends and calyces present an equally attractive appearance and others are valued for their outline.

The greatest problem in arranging individual fruits lies in persuading each item to remain in place and to lift it as you wish to see it. All kinds of little holders and supports can be used for this purpose, including flower pots, cream cartons, jars, egg cups, napkin rings and pastry cutters. These are easily hidden by leaves or other fruit. Alternatively, dry blocks of foamed plastic can be used instead or among these. It is possible gently but firmly to push objects into the plastic surface so that they make a depression shaped to their own contours which will hold them securely in place. Bunches of grapes and similar heavy clusters are best first tied or wired to a long, strong stem, which can then be arranged down into a stem holder in the usual manner.

Cherry Ripe

Regal lilies with croton and hosta leaves and cherries

1 Lilies bought in bud will open and mature in water. Those with many flowers to a stem can be thinned. The short-stemmed blooms are cut from them and used low in the arrangement. Use a large pinholder to anchor the heavy stems. Secure it to the container with pills of plasticine or adhesive clay.

2 Choose a slender stem for the centre. Cut away buds and blooms if there are more than two; a single blossom looks best. Measure the next stem so that its blooms do not hide the first. There can be more flowers and buds on this stem. Alternatively, use two stems each with a bloom and bud.

3 Repeat for the third stem. This can be well-flowered because it forms the body of the arrangement. Individual leaves should flow out from the centre so that they hide any stem ends and fill spaces. Later, arrange short-stemmed lilies and cherries tied in bunches to cocktail sticks which will act as stems.

Gold and Amber

Dahlias, golden rod, canary creeper, viburnum foliage and berries, and leycesteria foliage and berries

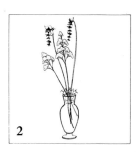

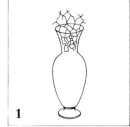

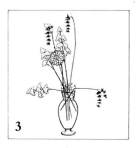

1 Vases of this shape are notoriously difficult to fill, yet they are very graceful. Ignore the main body of the vase and fill only the beaker-like top portion with large mesh wire-netting. Let a good proportion project above the vase to give support to the finer, slender stems.

2 The tallest stems should be slim. Set these as near to the back of the rim as possible. This leaves room for side and front stems. Tall back stems can be inserted right down vertically, or almost so, through the netting into the body of the vase.

3 Those stems which are placed at right angles to the centre will get enough water even if they only flow across the width of the top wire-filled portion. But if, when cutting them, stems which curve or are at any angle to the main stem are selected, the arrangement will be more effective. Be sure to top up the water level each day.

Edged with Lace

The white pedestal dish was not really deep enough to hold sufficient water to cover the large pin holder, so a deeper copper bowl was placed inside it. The carrot flower stems were divided, the largest umbels placed low and/or central

When vegetable plants go to seed the creative flower arranger may find unexpected bounty, for some of their flowers are handsome. Carrot, illustrated here, though common enough in the wild is rare in the well-ordered garden but beautiful enough to be treasured. Both kinds are so similar that they can be treated in the same way. All lacy umbels look particularly attractive with autumn fruits and coloured foliage. Garden carrot can be substituted by fennel or the smaller parsley, the wild flowers by hogweed, which often blooms late in the summer, especially when the waysides have been mown earlier.

The larger the umbels, the larger the fruits to complement them should be, or should only small berries be used as they are here, the greater the proportion. Berries provide a lively contrast to this type of flower. Heavily clustered berberis looks particularly well. So do the small kinds of grapes from ornamental vines such as 'Dusty Miller'. All the common

wild kinds are worth collecting, such as hips and haws and the beautiful blue sloes which cluster the thorn branches heavily in some seasons. Look also for viburnum, which of course also occurs in gardens and is very long lasting in arrangements.

Bryony, used here among the coloured viburnum leaves, grows in vines through the hedgerows, usually in abundance. It is as well to bear in mind that this particular berry is poisonous and should be kept away from small children. The fresh green glossy fruits and sagittate leaves look beautiful in summer flower and foliage arrangements.

Although the twisted stems are ideal for certain styles of arrangements they are seldom firm enough to stand upright. Like all twiners, the stem can be twisted around a different kind of stem quite effectively. Where the berries are to be massed low, the stems can be easily divided into shorter lengths which are then more rigid.

Bryony and hypericum fruits with carrot flowers and seed umbels, oats, honesty and viburnum and santolina foliage.

Late Summer

Roses, berberis, bryony, hypericum and rose species foliage in an old Staffordshire jug

1 Strip thorns from rose stem ends. Be sure to condition them. Fill the jug with large mesh wire-netting, cut ends uppermost, hooking two ends round the top of the handle to secure netting. Pull up cut ends at the back, to secure the tall stems of rose foliage and berberis, should this be necessary.

2 Arrange the tallest stems as near to the back of the container as possible, placing a tall, straight stem at the centre. If it is not tall enough, lift it by hooking a wire end round it. So long as the stem is in an inch of water, it will be all right. Remember to top up the jug daily.

3 Let the other stems all lean away from this straight stem. None should be seen to cross another. Give each rose room to expand. Remove any leaves which appear to be hiding the blooms, but do not take away so many that the character of the flowers is lost. Berries, recessed between the roses, add colour.

Leaf Textures

Iris seed pods, laurel and fading kale leaves, hydrangea, artichoke, unripe tomatoes and driftwood

1 Half fill the container with foamed plastic and top this with a mass of large mesh wire-netting. Mount small pieces of driftwood on 18-gauge florists' wire by making a loop at one end of the wire and laying this against the stem. Bring long end round both the wood and short leg twice.

2 Arrange the pieces of driftwood to make an interesting line which can later be followed by the other materials. Place heaviest pieces at lowest levels. Take the mount wires down through the wire-netting to the foam. Staple tomato bunch by hairpinning the stem with a length of bent wire.

3 Arrange glossy laurel leaves over the rim and at lower edges of the arrangement so that they will contrast with and frame the other lighter coloured and more varied materials. These can be removed if and when they fade while the main framework remains intact. Rhododendron leaves can be used as an alternative to laurel.

Galaxy

Formal dahlias are softened with sprays of snowberries (symphoricarpos), honesty and ornamental kale leaves

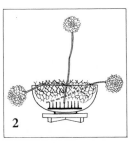

1 Dahlias are heavy flowers and must be firmly anchored. In this low bowl, a good mass of large mesh wire-netting is fixed on a heavy, large pinholder. The tallest stems are inserted through the netting and impaled on the holder. Protruding netting will give extra support.

2 This shows how it is done and also how the side stems are threaded through the wire. Foliage should be cut neatly from dahlia stems so that they are as smooth as possible, otherwise the snag ends will catch in the netting and make arrangement more difficult.

3 When fairly uniform flowers of one kind are to be arranged, it is advisable to recess some of them at lower levels to give depth to the arrangement. A few buds set among them give a lighter touch. Stems placed low down so they flow out over the rim give a three-dimensional effect.

September Souvenir

Glowing viburnum berries attractively associated with dahlias and gladioli in a modern-style arrangement

1 This attractive vase stands firm and is ideal for an arrangement in which heavy flowers are to be used. It has an edge round the rim under which wire-netting can be pushed to keep it firm. Even so, the cut ends are brought to the centre for extra support.

2 Flowers are grouped, although not too strictly, in zones. The first stems are important because they set the size and the style of the arrangement. Lower leaves should be stripped from the gladiolus stems but saved and used later; the stems will be too bulky if they are left on.

3 Work from the top down to the lower levels and centre. As the flowers are selected, set aside those which are obviously best for placement at rim level. Later, some leaves will need pruning from the sprays of viburnum to display the berries. It is often best to bunch and tie short-stemmed clusters together before arrangement.

Sunset

Golden conifer foliage, andromeda, mahonia, physalis or Chinese lanterns, holly berries and tangerines in Poole pottery

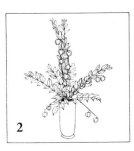

1 Cut a piece of large mesh wire-netting twice the height of the container and a little wider. Fold it into a U and put it into the vase with cut ends uppermost. These can be used to hook round a difficult stem or even to pin leaves in place.

2 Define the height and width of the arrangement first, and then work towards the centre. Taper the materials by using the most slender at the highest points. Either use large pieces, or mass several smaller ones together at the lower levels. Low flowing stems give good balance to the design.

3 Physalis should be cut just when the first lanterns are changing colour. Remove all foliage. Short stems can be lengthened by inserting a florists' wire in their base; they will then hang more gracefully. The wires should not show. Mount tangerines by passing a wire under the skin but not into the flesh.

Soft and Subtle

Sprays of pernettya and symphoricarpos berries with lichen-covered branches show that fruits can be as lovely as flowers

1 Berry sprays like leafy branches need to be carefully trimmed. Cut away all damaged growth and strip stem ends for easy arrangement. Save lower side growths both for furnishing the vase and hiding the stem holder. Well-soaked foamed plastic is used here for a stem holder. Alternatively, use wire-netting.

2 Group short, heavily-berried clusters over the tim. The plastic holds the stems firmly so there is no need to insert them very far into the vase. If possible, when removing side stems from branches, also cut a little of the main branch so, when positioned, these will flow roughly at right angles to their stem.

3 Recess some of the berries and leaves to give depth and contour to the arrangement. This is always a good thing to do when mainly one kind of flower or material is used, because it takes the place of contrasting material and adds interest to the design.

Foliage Patterns

If you have no flowers, look for leaves instead. Arrangements made entirely of foliage can be extremely beautiful and they are usually very long lasting in comparison with flowers. You can specialise and select just one kind of leaf and play a variation on that, or you can mix and vary the foliage just as you might a vase of flowers. It is possible to create wonderful colour harmonies from leaves in which little green need appear.

The same rules we follow for flower arrangement still apply when leafy materials are being assembled. The most effective monochromatic arrangements are those with strong contrasts of materials. Emphasis on contrast can be provided by using driftwood, burned gorse, ivy root and bare branches. Subjects used to sketch outlines and provide height and line can vary from these to branches, fern fronds, rushes and grasses.

Compact shapes for the centres need to be well defined. The terminal cluster of leaves on some stems, rhododendrons for example, is often flower-like in form and can be used as a focal point. It is possible to group individual leaves in much the same manner. Sometimes entire plants can be used, even one growing in a pot if the arrangement and its container are large enough. Alternatively, knock the plant from its pot and secure its rootball in a

polythene bag to protect it from becoming waterlogged in the container, or use whole rosettes of sempervivums or houseleeks, or of London pride, both of which resemble great chunky flowers. Their stems usually need lengthening or supporting. Cocktail sticks can be inserted up inside the succulent stems. Those of London pride are best lashed to a fine twig or robust straw, otherwise they are difficult to coax down inside a container. Also flower-like are ornamental or 'flower' cabbage and little red pickling kinds shown in 'Rose Contrast' (page 107).

Dense umbels of carrot, parsley, celery, angelica and similar umbellifers also look well at the centre of an arrangement. Those which are of a more open pattern are best placed at the edges of an arrangement so that they can be seen outlined against their background.

While they may not be strictly foliage, parts of some plants are leafy in appearance and are decorative and worth saving. These include calyces of cobaea, primulas, carnations, dahlias and daisies. Seed stems and seed heads as well as immature blossoms and fruits can all be grouped under the foliage banner, although if the arrangement is to be entered for a competition it would be prudent first to study the schedule carefully in case flowers and fruits, however immature, are barred.

Touched with Silver – *surrounded by silvery cytisus, stachys, senecio and achillea, a group of chunky succulent rosettes take the place of true flowers.*

Colour Harmony

Coleus cuttings with driftwood

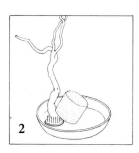

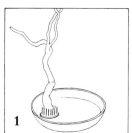

1 This background can be permanent and used time and time again to supplement whatever plant materials or flowers are available. The burned gorse is impaled firmly on a pinholder which has itself also been fixed to the floor of the container with small clay pills.

2 A cylinder of foamed plastic is tilted against the base of the gorse. This will hold fresh stems as well as small pot plants, which can also be used in an arrangement of this kind. Press the base of the pots into the stem holder. However, a pinholder alone may also be used, as shown.

3 A piece of driftwood curved round the foam hides the pinholder from view. Alternatively, bark, stones or pebbles may be used but space should be left so that the coleus cuttings can be easily arranged. Once the cuttings are in position, the dish should be topped up daily with water.

Rose Contrast

Red cabbages and catkins, with Sterling Silver roses, show that each has much in common with the other

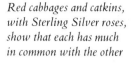

1 Place the pinholder to the back of the low bowl to allow the maximum space for the larger lower cabbage and its surrounding leaves. See that the holder is really firm before beginning to arrange the materials, because cabbages are heavier than most flowers.

2 Catkin stems usually need pruning. In this case, the long stems on the left of the branch have been cut away. These can always be trimmed and used at low levels. Cut cabbages with long stems. Alternatively pull them up by the roots.

3 Taper the line of cabbages by arranging the smallest at the tip, even removing some of the leaves from the tallest to get this effect. These can be arranged low behind the large cabbage to add bulk to it should this be necessary. Make sure that the stems are firmly anchored.

Spring Greens

Horse chestnut, maple and guelder rose (viburnum) with doronicum seed heads and other green foliage in a white Wedgwood vase

1 Tall branches of blossom are often top-heavy, so it is important to provide a heavy stem holder. Use a pinholder which fits snugly into the base of the container. Fix it by using pills of plasticine or adhesive clay pressed on to its dry base. Push the holder down on the dry floor of the container and it will hold firm.

2 On this, impale large mesh wire-netting to support the individual leaves and finer stems. Before arranging stems of viburnum blooms, test them in the hand to gauge the way they tend to flow and arrange them accordingly. Remove side branches from the lower part of the stems.

3 Keep all the small side portions to arrange at the back of the vase to help wedge the tallest stems and also to hide the stem holder. Recess short pieces of blossom, and horse chestnut and other foliage. Top up with tepid water after arrangement.

Garden Gleanings

Poppy and parsley seed heads, bryony berries, hazel nuts, with grasses, honesty and mixed foliage

1 Fill the vase with large mesh wire-netting, drawing up the cut ends to stand well above the rim level so that they can support slender stems. It should reach to the bottom of the container. Large mesh, $1\frac{1}{2}$ to 2 in (4 to 5 cm), is much more malleable than a smaller mesh.

2 'Sketch' in the outline of the arrangement. Put the tallest centre stem in place first. Let the smallest or finest materials be at the top and the rounder, heavier ones at the lower levels. Strip stem ends so that they are inserted easily.

3 Work from the edges to the centre and from the top to the rim. Group materials but do not zone them too strictly. Soft greys and shining white help different hues to merge prettily. Bryony stems are cut into lengths with berry clusters at the tip. Other green berries may be used instead.

Seed Stem Shapes

At first glance this arrangement appears to be a very leafy one, but closer inspection proves that it is the base which is formed of leaves, palmate fatsia and variegated maple. The rest are flowers and seed stems, but being mainly green they strike a leafy note.

As in the previous chapter, our attention is directed to the beauty of homely vegetable flowers. These leeks, some of which were soft, silvery grey-green and others soft lavender when in full flower, have turned to seed but kept their hues in softly muted tones. These are so decorative and so long lasting that it is well worth the gardener's time to allow a few of the food plants to flower.

They look lovely moved from the kitchen garden to a flower border or in an area devoted to silver grey plants and grown in groups. If the leeks are given plenty of growing space they all will produce large heads. For variety it is best to allow a few plants to grow close together to produce heads of different sizes.

Stems are always long and firm. The portions cut away from large heads arranged low down are worth saving, for they serve as false stems for large leaves and for some of the heavy perpetuelles such as lotus seed heads and others which are marketed stemless or virtually so. The same flowers can be used time and time again, first with fresh materials and later with dried.

As you would expect, large, handsome leaves suit these great rounded shapes. Fallen brown fatsia and other great leaves such as some rhododendrons and magnolias can be sponged clean, dried and then sprayed with a leaf gloss or lacquer. Alternatively, they can be lightly oiled, but the disadvantage here being that in time the oil holds dust and so dulls the colours.

Although the leeks are grown outdoors, the flowers look beautiful when arranged with certain tender house plants, particularly with

Begonia rex and cordyline, whose lovely hues can be found in those of the flowers or seed heads.

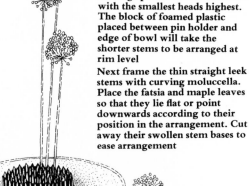

Arrange the tall, heavy leek flowers first of all to ensure that their stems are firmly impaled on the large pin holder. Grade them with the smallest heads highest. The block of foamed plastic placed between pin holder and edge of bowl will take the shorter stems to be arranged at rim level

Next frame the thin straight leek stems with curving moluccella. Place the fatsia and maple leaves so that they lie flat or point downwards according to their position in the arrangement. Cut away their swollen stem bases to ease arrangement

Globular leek, fennel umbels, quilled phlomis, pearly honesty and shell-like moluccella, with fatsia, maple and flag foliage.

Herb Patch

Purple and golden variegated sage, pineapple mint, rue, lavender and parsley seed heads

1 Push cylinder of soaked foamed plastic into a mortar or similarly shaped container. Alternatively, use some other kitchen utensil – a copper jelly mould or coloured saucepan. Let the stem holder protrude above rim so that small pieces of herbs can be easily and profitably arranged. Insert the tallest stem so that its tip comes roughly above the centre of the container.

2 Prune side branches from this stem until it is slender and well-proportioned. Cut pieces neatly away close to the main stem. Arrange the tallest side stem upright, in line with the central first stem. Use others as 'edge' stems and for filling (see drawing 3). Recess the seed heads between leafy pieces at lower levels.

3 Group lavender sprigs and arrange rue, placing side stems of parsley among them and at the extremities. Later, arrange sprigs of sage, trimming off lower leaves if these appear cumbersome.

Centrepiece

An assortment of preserved and fresh materials sets an easily-followed pattern for a table decoration

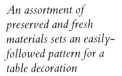

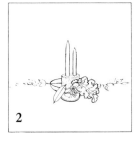

1 The modern stem-holding materials make flower arranging so easy! A block of foamed plastic securely holds two candles and flower stems. If pinholders are used instead, first fix them in position, then heat them by pouring hot water over them so that the candles will slip on easily. Allow pinholders to cool before positioning flowers. Side stems should flow horizontally.

2 If the arrangement is to be oval in shape, the stems to the back and front will not need to be as long as those at the two side stems. So let these flow down a little over the rim of the container. Kale and cabbage leaves are easier to arrange if a cocktail stick is first inserted in the base of the thick stem.

3 Intermediate stems sketch the shape of the arrangement. When using foamed plastic for fresh flowers, leave room between it and the sides of the container, then top up the water daily. Leafy arrangements last best if they are sprayed occasionally with clear water.

Old and New

Preserved leaves with newly-cut twigs, ivy and variegated kale

1 A long-lasting framework of preserved leaves can be dressed up with living material as it becomes available. This may be renewed as required, the preserved leaves remaining in place. Use a base of foamed plastic covered with water and topped with wire-netting. The ends of preserved stems should not sit too deeply in the water.

2 Arrange the preserved beech in a roughly triangular pattern. Strip stem ends but carefully save side branches. Use very short pieces to hide the stem holder and to contrast with the unpreserved leaves which will be placed between them. Side branches cut with some of the main stem should flow downwards gracefully.

3 Trails and individual leaves of variegated ivy are placed between and before the beech. Alternatively, use variegated periwinkle or any other graceful variegated material. Let some trails flow over the rim of the vase. Place the longest and brightest leaves near the centre for contrast. Pass the stems through the wire-netting and water into the soaked plastic foam.

114

Stars and Shells

Mussel shells brought back from a Spanish holiday, driftwood or burned gorse and varied cryptanthus

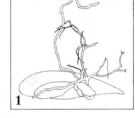

1 An outsize Spanish mussel shell acts as both base and container. Small pieces of driftwood or burned gorse can be anchored either by inserting them in a block of plasticine or in adhesive clay. An attractive piece of cork bark and the ends of the smaller shells hide the holder.

2 Trim the branches if these are over-fussy. Wedge a cryptanthus (earth star) in place. (These plants can be watered merely by spraying the leaves with water daily.) Arrange another shell in line with the driftwood accentuating its curve. Wedge shells in place with pebbles or with more clay.

3 Arrange other plants according to their hue or pattern. Turn each one so that it faces outwards displaying its form. This also helps to conceal the plant pots. Pebbles or sea shells can be used to lift the pots to the correct angle so that lower leaves are not bruised or damaged.

Plants and Flowers

If you have sometimes wished that the beauty and presence of the arrangements you make from cut flowers were not quite so fleeting, consider sometimes making decorations in which entire living plants are used. Bowls, baskets, troughs and many other kinds of vessels can be filled at any season of the year with a mixture of plants. These arrangements can be quite as attractive in their own way as any vase of blooms.

Naturally the plants must still be cared for while they are arranged this way. If you use blocks of foamed plastic stem holder to lift, wedge or tilt various pots, this can be kept damp and so will generate the necessary humidity around the plants. An atomiser is enough to water any bromeliad you use, while others will need inspecting every few days to make sure that they have not become dry at their roots.

It is not a great step from arranging several plants together to another fascinating method of arrangement. By combining these plants with a few cut flowers and natural accessories you can assemble *pot et fleur* arrangements which offers you a delightful and distinctive way of decorating a house. The illustrations of *pot et fleur* in this chapter demonstrate clearly that the minimum of flowers is often all that is required.

The same plants can frequently be used

Exotic Beauties – *long-lasting cymbidium orchids with dried yucca pods and two species of dracaena and cryptanthus, their pots hidden by gnarled driftwood*

time and time again, although generally speaking the plant arrangement portion of the ensemble should be long-lived enough for you to change the flowers only. When the plants become jaded and depending upon how green are your fingers, they can be rested and restored, but even if they have to be thrown away they will have proved to be better value than a bunch of flowers.

Colour harmony offers few problems. If only green plants are to be used one can rest assured that any flower will harmonise with them. On the other hand, many pot plants, even those which have no flowers, have many more colours and hues than green in them. Sometimes stems, stipules, tendrils or the undersides of the leaves are remarkably coloured and well worth accentuating in some way. The fun then lies in finding the flowers – or the fruits or other foliage – to match or harmonise with them. When two or three plants are to be used these can also be harmonised, although this is not essential.

Generally speaking, any containers used need to be wide. You need accessories not only for completing the arrangement but also for masking the pots and the vessels you use to hold the flowers. The line drawings which accompany the illustrations show how these elements are used.

Early Spring

Pretty primroses and hyacinths, either pot grown or lifted from the garden, can be arranged with trailing house plants

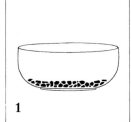

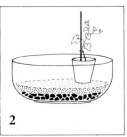

1 There is no need for drainage holes in bowls for plant arrangements, but there should be a good layer of drainage material, such as crushed charcoal, small shingle or flower-pot crocks. Charcoal also keeps the soil sweet because it absorbs gases from water which may lie at the bottom of the bowl.

2 Before transplanting primroses into the pot soil, 'plant' the pots of ivy and tradescantia. See that the tops of the pots fall below the rim of the bowl. Cover them with soil or compost. In deep bowls, adjust height by placing soil or drainage material or even foamed plastic below the pot.

3 Hyacinths can be transplanted from boxes or pots too. They can also sometimes be bought 'on bulb'. If the pots of trailing and scrambling plants, such as tradescantia, are slightly tilted, the trails will cascade prettily over the rim of the bowl, but make certain that the plant can still be watered.

Green Sculpture

Pot et fleur of sansevieria, hedera (ivy), peperomia and tulips arranged with hosta leaves and driftwood

1 Sansevieria is the tallest 'stem' in this arrangement. Its pot stands upright on the bottom of the bowl packed in by peat, soil, sand, moss or even used foamed plastic. Turn and study the plant to get the best view of the line of its leaves.

2 Large-leaved ivy has been unfastened from its stake and one trail grows up, while the other, held down by driftwood, cascades prettily. The peperomia is raised by slipping its pot inside another smaller one. This is both held in place and hidden by another piece of driftwood.

3 The vase, for the flowers and the hosta leaves, first has a pinholder fixed inside. Alternatively, large mesh wire-netting can be used. It is then arranged upright, near the rim of the container, but well inside it so that no water will over-flow on to the table. Finally arrange the tulips.

Get-Well Gift

Hyacinth and double tulips with aconites and chlorophytum

1 It is fun to watch the flowers on bulbs and roots grow, so make an arrangement like this while all are still in bud, or very young. Line a basket with polythene or cooking foil to make it water-tight. Add two cream cartons for the cut flowers.

2 The bulbs can be packed in place with moist, used bulb fibre, peat, used foamed plastic, moss or soil. Put the tallest in first. Make sure that these stand well. If they tend to be top-heavy, either wedge them in place with stones, or (and this is less weighty) put each bulb in a cream carton or small flower pot.

3 Arrange the plant in its pot, this will also help to wedge the tall hyacinths in place. Cover the surface with fresh moss. Make sure that none trails over the edge of the basket or it may act as a siphon. Finally, fill the cartons with well-soaked foamed plastic and arrange the flowers. Place driftwood or bark in the centre.

Mother's Day

An African violet with hazel and willow catkins, white heather, snowdrops, crocuses, ivy trails and begonia leaves in a mixing bowl

1 A gift that is long-lasting as well as pretty! The container is a mixing bowl, which is always useful. The crocuses can be planted in the garden to bloom again. The begonia leaves and ivy trails can be rooted later in water. Fill the bowl with a block of soaked foamed plastic or use moist sand or peat.

2 Push the plant pot into the foam at the side of the bowl. Tilt pot to· show the flowers to advantage. Arrange tall stems of catkins, trimming to keep them compact where necessary. Make depressions in the foam with a spoon for the crocus bulbs and arrange.

3 Push the begonia leaves into the foam. Arrange ivy trails over these. Group white heather behind the saintpaulia so that it shows from the front. Finally, arrange the snowdrops one by one, pushing their stems down between the other materials.

Natural Simplicity

Pot et fleur with dracaena, cordyline, starry cryptanthus and tulips, which can be changed for other spring flowers as they fade

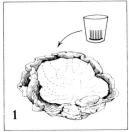

1 The container is really a large dried oyster fungus, found growing on a tree, lined with polythene to make it watertight. Alternatively, a large clam shell or a wicker basket could be used. The latter would also need lining. Cut or tuck in lining just below rim level to hide it.

2 Arrange the driftwood. Wedge both this and the pot containing the tall dracaena in place with stones or pebbles. Place a pinholder in a little vessel and place this in position ready for the tulips. It must be possible to remove this for cleaning and replacing when flowers are changed.

3 Tilt the cryptanthus. Water this later by spraying daily with an atomiser. It is not essential to water its roots if it is sprayed. Wedge it in place using soil, peat, moss, foamed plastic, stones or driftwood. The latter can also be used to hide pots and flower containers.

Golden Glow

A glowing pot et fleur composed of *Gudoshnik tulips, crotons, hedera, sansevieria and cryptanthus*

1 A lampstand has a bowl fitted in the top to hold the plants. The tall croton is the only vertical plant. The rest are tilted at various angles so that they flow away from the centre. They also hide the metal cones in which the flowers are placed.

2 As the plants are assembled, wedge them in position with stones and driftwood, after first raising and supporting them with soil, peat, compost, foamed plastic or moss. See that all of these materials are kept constantly moist but not sodden.

3 See that the metal cones to hold the flowers are properly hidden. These must stand upright or the water will be spilled. Cones in various sizes can be bought from any florists' sundriesman. Trails of ivy can be gently pulled low and held down by stones or driftwood.

Pot et Fleur Sec

Fit a block of foamed plastic into the bottom of a wide bowl. Place the tall sansevieria in position first. Press all pot bases lightly down into the plastic so they are held in place. Fit more plastic pieces around the pots to hold the stems of the perpetuelles. Arrange the tallest stems at the back of the arrangement between the pots

Pot et fleur arrangements are ideal for winter decorations, especially where they are to decorate cosy environments. Most of the house plants we use are house-hardy and so long as they are watered and given a little humidity they should go on growing for many days. The cut flowers used with them, on the other hand, may fade very quickly, especially if they are really hardy, spring-flowering kinds such as daffodils. Other flowers also fade, perhaps not quite so quickly but too fast to be economic.

This being the case, why not turn attention to dried flower or perpetuelle substitutes? These may not be so colourful, but many are extremely handsome. If the thought of mixing living and dried flowers is not at first appealing, think of the many examples we all see around us of new life showing through that which is past and faded, of corn stubble with the fresh green grass pushing through it, or of the tufted bluebell shoots and early dog's mercury growing through the blanket of dried fallen beech leaves. Each have their own

beauty which many people find deeply satisfying. We can apply the same ecological theme to winter *pot et fleur*.

Of course, it cannot be expressed in such simple terms in floristry. We have first and foremost to consider the practical angle, but like so much that we have examined in this book it can serve as an inspiration.

If we turn to dried materials because the arrangement we plan is to stand in a hot, dry environment, we need also to consider what plants will survive in these conditions. The great, glowing neoregelia in the arrangement illustrated is just one of a fascinating family of bromeliads, cousins of the pineapple and sometimes known as room pines. Many are highly decorative. The cryptanthus used in the chapter opening illustration of this chapter is also a bromeliad.

They all take water in a very simple manner – in the centre cup or urn made by the overlapping bases of their leaves. This little reservoir should be kept constantly filled, an easy matter if you use an atomiser. At the same time this can be used to spray and keep happy the leaves of any other plants used, even though these will be watered through their roots. Those that will tolerate the same conditions are the house palms and sansevieria, both used here.

Grouped around a glowing neoregelia are potted cocos palm and sansevieria and dried cocoa 'boats', lotus seed heads and agave stems.

Cool Elegance

Pot et fleur with glorious pink paeonies, arranged in bud and allowed to open, with sansevieria, ivy, scindapsus and sedum

1 Arrange the tall sansevieria. Its pot rim should be just below the rim of the container. Should it protrude, it can be hidden later but make sure that water will not spill from it. Fill the paeony container with wire-netting. See that it stands upright. Add water later.

2 Arrange ivy plant. Untie and gently pull some trails away from its stake so that they scramble prettily. Tilt the sedum a little so that it flows over the edge and its rim is hidden. Wedge pots in place with soil, peat, foamed plastic, moss, stones or driftwood.

3 Extra leaves or flowers, in a *pot et fleur*, can be arranged in an empty tablet tube pushed down among the plant pots. Little cuttings of ivy, tradescantia and others will root this way and can be potted later. For tall arrangements, tubes may be fastened to thin stakes or plant stems.

126

Vine Plants

Sand–blasted vine root with Philodendron melanochrysum *and fittonias*

1 Such a heavy piece of wood must be well anchored. A good method is to use cross pieces of angle iron as a foot and to screw the wood in place. First find which way the root tends to stand. Driftwood and burned gorse can also be used like this.

2 Strew the base of the container with charcoal nuggets to keep the soil or compost sweet. Carefully knock the creeper from its pot and place it in position. Plants may be kept in their pots if these are shallower than the container. Fasten the creeper to the wood.

3 Arrange the two fittonias at the foot of the philodendron. Cover their roots with soil or compost and fill the rest of the container. Water to settle the soil. Cover the surface with moss. Alternatively, use chippings, aquaria stones or tiny shells. Keep arrangement in the light but out of strong sunlight.

Everlasting Flowers

Dried flowers and other kinds of dried plant materials, which collectively I have named perpetuelles, make an important contribution to modern indoor decoration, especially in winter.

It is unfortunate that to some people the description 'dried' should conjure up a vision of lifeless, shabby, even dusty relics of a plant, for perpetuelles need never appear so. The illustrations of my arrangements shown in this chapter surely demonstrate how lively as well as how extremely varied dried flowers can be.

Modern examples differ greatly from the dried bouquets of the past century which bedecked drawing rooms and mantelpieces in winter. These became the rage once the native Australian helichrysums and other straw daisies were introduced to astonished gardeners on this side of the world. They looked lovely enough when newly arranged, but due to dust and smoke from coal fires the arrangements which should have coloured the winter days instead soon became shabby and dirty as the weeks passed by. No wonder that after a time many people who claimed that they were dust-traps refused to have them in their homes.

Another cause of their decline in popular favour was the growth of the greenhouse industry. An increasing number of commercially-grown flowers, once the

Chinese Lanterns – *some physalis pods have been cut along the veins and opened out to make orange 'flowers'. With them are achillea and honesty*

prerogative of the rich, were produced out of season and sold quite cheaply. This being the case, who would wish to retain a dusty mass of statice, grasses and straw flowers in early spring once it was possible to replace them with a cheap bunch of fresh daffodils?

Gradually the dried bouquets vanished from the scene, only to return decades later in a new form and for a completely different reason. Dried flower arrangements are now not only acceptable and fashionable, but also both decorative and practical. Where winter heat in the form of dust-creating open fires once drove them out of favour, modern centrally-heated homes have been responsible for their renaissance. In winter many of today's homes are often heated to such an extent that the air is too dry for cut flowers to last more than a day or two, yet perpetuelles will endure, even when stood upon a night storage heater or on a shelf over a radiator. Here they may in time become brittle, but if treated carefully they can be left on display for months, or in my own experience, for years.

A further point – gas, oil lamps and candles were the source of light when dried flowers first became popular. This meant that except when the sun shone directly upon them, these decorations were never seen at their best. Lighting in modern interiors is now so adaptable that even the slightest nuance of hue can be exploited. Dried materials of any kind can be made to appear much more lively than they really are. With good lighting those arrangements which are devoid of spectrum colours can still be most attractive, for the creative flower arranger should be able to emphasise other features, drawing attention perhaps to shapes and textures as well as exploiting the lovely silhouettes of skeletal forms.

As one would expect, the styles of dried arrangements as well as the contents can be as varied as those made of fresh flowers, each design being influenced by the type of materials from which it has been assembled. It is possible to buy many unusual and exotic materials, some of them, such as lotus seed heads, quite large. In the average home these can be used to create eye-catching still-life groups. Sometimes one or more can form the focal point of an arrangement in which homely garden-grown and native materials are used as well.

Those who have gardens can grow some of the favourite true flowers usually classed as everlastings, for many are half-hardy annuals and easily cultivated. These include helichrysum or straw daisies, so called because of their stiff, straw-like petals, in white, yellow, orange and red analogous harmonies. Acroclinium, more like large field daisies, are softer petalled, sweet scented when fresh and with stronger straight stems, which unlike those of the helichrysum remain attached to the flower head. Closely related rhodanthe are daintier still, with pendent blooms and very fine stems. Statice or limonium have long branching stems and contribute blue and purple, pink and white as well as yellow. The latter should always be gathered when all the flowers on the stem are seen to be mature. The others, the 'daisies', should be picked as soon as they open. All should be hung head downwards in a dry, dark place, in well spaced little bunches until they have dried.

Grasses, most of which are hardy and half hardy annuals are also easy to grow. These include bromas, briza, hare's-tail and squirrel-tail grasses and the lovely Job's tears. Gather all of these while they are still young and dry, like the flowers, away from the light.

Certain perennial garden flowers can also be cut and dried. All of them lose a little intensity of colour after drying and then continue to fade slowly as they grow older (the true everlastings keep their colours much better) even so they are well worth using for they contribute contrasting shapes as well as colours and textures not found in the others. These need drying fast in a warm, dry, dark place. I use an airing cupboard. The best of them are acanthus, achillea, alchemilla, bistort, delphinium and larkspur, solidago or golden rod, paeonies, hydrangeas and some roses. The exciting thing is that once you become interested in drying flowers you discover new kinds, often by accident. For instance, flowers may dry in an arrangement you failed to keep topped up with water. Some seasons appear to be more productive than others, when flowers such as zinnias and double sunflowers, scarlet salvias and others dry easily.

Also perennial are the bright orange physalis seed pods, known as Chinese lanterns because of their characteristic shape. These stay in good form and colour for a year or two. Similar in shape, not so colourful perhaps but worthy of interest, are the seed vessels of the annual *Nicandra physaloides*, a good garden plant. Another old favourite are the silvery stems of the round, satiny seed pods of honesty. Though often seen arranged on its own, honesty is something which appears to harmonise delightfully with everything, fresh, dried or still growing. Honesty should be gathered early in the season, as soon as you can see that the flat seeds inside the round pods are mature. Either cut the stems or pull up the entire plant to hang upside down in some dry place. When you can easily pull the outer parts away from the central 'moon', it is ready for arrangement.

Pine and larch cones look like and can be treated as wooden flowers. These are so easily obtained. Just search the ground under the trees. Larch cones are produced on graceful branches and are clustered generously. Individual cones of all kinds can be mounted on false stems of wire.

There are many wild seed heads decorative enough to be included in dried arrangements, often usefully providing essential tall lines and graceful shapes at the extremities of a mass of other perpetuelles. Umbellifers such as hedge parsley and hogweed are best picked before their seeds become really ripe, although even the bare umbels have a special ethereal beauty, in particular if they are seen against the light. Wild carrot flower, garden fennel and other dense umbels can be picked in bloom and then dried. The umbels will close during this process, but they can be gently coaxed open again by firm, gentle smoothing with the fingers. Some dried thistle seed heads make attractive, starry focal points. If these have to be given false stems, hold the prickly flower in a cloth as you wire or otherwise elongate the stem.

Wild clematis, *C. vitalba*, and some other species which also have long, fluffy, feathery seed styles, are delightful in appearance and so useful for contrasting and softening the thicker shapes and textures of some of the denser, heavier materials. This, like many kinds of foliage, keeps its form best if preserved.

All of them are dependent on being gathered at the right moment. Clematis should still be green, foliage such as beech should be just ready to turn colour, evergreens such as laurel and elaeagnus should be mature. To preserve,

split their stem ends and stand them for conditioning in about 2 in (5 cm) of boiling water. Allow them to remain in this as it cools and for at least twelve hours so you can see that the branches are taking water well. Discard any with curled leaves. Then prepare a mixture of one part glycerine to two parts boiling water and stand the conditioned stems in this. When they are properly charged with the solution the leaves or styles will change colour and be of a more silky texture. They should then be taken out and stored ready for use.

If you study the illustrations of the arrangements featured in this chapter, you will see that most of them contain perpetuelles which have been massed. Generally speaking this style of arrangement is best, simply because in the mass many of the more fragile perpetuelles are well supported by their own kinds. There are many ways of aiding the arrangement of even the most unlikely materials. Stems can be lengthened or strengthened and stem holders can be exploited to lend height. These aids are illustrated in some of the line drawings which accompany the photographs or are explained in the captions in this chapter.

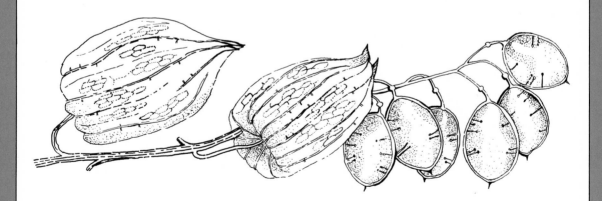

Symphony

A mixture of wild and garden materials, pressed bracken, briza grass, honesty, wild clematis and helipterums in a pottery mug

1 Many of these materials are very short stemmed and do not penetrate far into the mug. To give extra height, a cylinder of florists' foam, which just fits into the mouth of the mug, is kept well above the rim. Some stems can be inserted into the sides of the foam cylinder.

2 Bracken fonds should be divided. The side branches used here are quite large enough for the average arrangement. Cut whole fronds as soon as they begin to turn colour, long before the frost affects them, and press between newspaper under a weight. Some side fronds will need false stems.

3 Even if they are on false stems, insert the tallest materials deepest into the stem holder to make sure they are held firm and will not move position. When using containers with handles, an attractive line is made if the curve follows the same direction as the handle.

132

Pot-pourri

Helichrysums – as one would expect in a dried arrangement – but also hydrangea, senecio buds and roses

1 Stiff yet slender stemmed helichrysums and tumbling hydrangeas need different styles of stem holders. Place a layer of gravel at the bottom, then a layer of foamed plastic to take the tall slender stems. Press some large mesh wire-netting onto the foam. The cut ends of wire can be hooked round hydrangea stems so that they can be pulled low.

2 Most of these tall flowers need false stems to lengthen them and it is best to get these in position first. Hydrangea heads can be divided and the clusters mounted on false stems or wires to give smaller blooms for the higher levels or the extremities.

3 Sketch the outline, working from the edges to the centre. Place the first stems as near to the back of the vase as possible to leave plenty of room for the larger materials which are arranged later. Note where false stems are likely to show and choose other tapering stems to hide these.

Tone Poem

Eucalyptus and grevillea from the flower shop, with acroclinium, senecio buds, hypericum seed heads, toadstool 'lilies' and cones

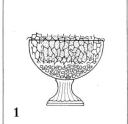

1 Shallow containers need extra weighting for this style of arrangement. Because stems vary so much in thickness, the stem holder is also varied. Gravel for weight, a core of foamed plastic for the tall stems, and wire-netting protruding above the rim to support the slender seed head stems.

2 Curving grevillea defines the height and general style of the arrangement. This has been well pruned, side branches cut away are used lower down. Eucalyptus is preserved by being stood in glycerine and water solution for just forty-eight hours. Individual leaves cut from the pointed leaf form are used at rim level.

3 Arrange the main central part of the arrangement first. The silvery dried senecio buds give height and the daisies are massed to give a flowery effect among the leaves. Cone 'roses' are made by fixing individual cones on a fabric ring round a small central cone. Dried toadstool 'flowers' are threaded on strong straws.

Pot of Gold

Preserved beech and pressed hardy geranium leaves make a good frame for golden helichrysum and solidago

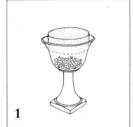

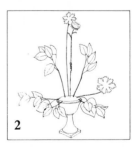

1 When a fairly shallow vase is used for a large tall arrangement use a block of foamed plastic as a stem holder and let it protrude above the rim of the container to the required height. See that it fits tightly and will not move. The vase should first be weighted with gravel or sand.

2 Hardy geranium leaves retain their stems when pressed between newspaper under a weight, but they may need lengthening by using florists' wires. Alternatively, stick straws to them with a quick-drying adhesive. The tallest helichrysums are also mounted on wires. Slender, stiff stems penetrate this type of stem holder easily.

3 Arrange the straw daisies, trying to give the impression that all the stems flow from the centre point: this will help to give a natural effect. Eliminate the inevitable stiffness of dried flowers by slightly curving some of the wire stems or wires inserted into the base of the stems.

Winter Plumage

Ornamental grasses of all kinds, some of which are easily grown, some of which can be bought and some of which grow wild, and farm cereals such as oats, wheat and barley, are of great value to those who create decorations from perpetuelles. Apart from their individual beauty – and they are quite lovely enough to be used in place of flowers – they so often bring to a mixture the exact shape, texture or atmosphere to create a pleasing harmony. They fill in the spaces between other kinds of materials without adding weight or density. Those which are of a pendent or arching habit contrast prettily with the inevitably stiff stems of certain of the everlastings.

However, while these medium-size grasses are useful in so many ways, some people find that the great plumes of the larger grasses, such as the outsize and popular pampas or cortaderia, although so striking and beautiful, are not so easy to apply to home decorations. These are denser, with stronger forms, thicker colour and textures. Even used in very large arrangements they tend to dominate the other flowers with which they are placed and the results are too often unsatisfactory.

The secret is to use these large, heavy grasses as the main fabric in an arrangement rather than as an embellishment or a supplement to blooms and foliage. Let them dictate the shape and style of the arrangement and once this is established fit in those materials you wish to use with them.

Obviously the very long stems have to be considerably shortened. This being the case, usually the inflorescence or plume needs to be lessened in some way so that it appears to be in proportion. By dividing the plumes you can make them appear to be less dense.

All of those in the arrangement illustrated have been reduced by pulling away either whole sections of the plume or smaller pieces throughout its length. This way you can tailor

Strip the ends of the grass stems so that they are slim and clean. Push them into the protruding portion of the foamed plastic and down deep enough to keep them quite firmly anchored at the required angle. Next fill in the spaces with fern. The two lowest fronds of dark fern and other short low-growing pieces should be pushed into the face of the foamed plastic. Point their stem ends towards the centre of the vase

smaller plumes more suitable for the tips or edges of the arrangement. Here, some of the shorter pieces pulled away have been arranged at the lowest levels. Very small pieces may be set aside to use as individual grasses in smaller arrangements.

Creamy, silky pampas grass, brown and white pressed ferns, silvery honesty and bleached artichoke flowers in a matching creamy white vase.

Summer Remembered

Acroclinium, rhodanthe, statice and blue hydrangea demonstrate that perpetuelles can be as gay as a summer border

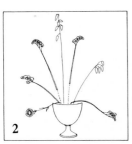

1 So many and such tall flowers need firm anchoring. Make allowances for all the types of stem and false stems. Wire netting is pressed into a layer of foamed plastic and this rests on a layer of gravel which weights the container and prevents the arrangement from overbalancing.

2 Many of the tallest stems have been artificially lengthened. It is possible to insert a florists' wire into the thick stems of statice, but thinner side stems have to be mounted. Alternatively, stems can be spliced to thick grass straws with narrow adhesive tape, in some cases, thicker drinking straws can be used.

3 Statice is very branching and often too dense and heavy to be used in its natural state. Cut away side stems to use lower down. Leave the top, nicely-shaped spray, for tall positions and the extremities of an arrangement. Pull grasses up and out to display their inflorescences.

Brown Study

An arrangement like this is built up slowly and thoughtfully, like a picture, as materials are collected

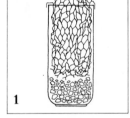

1 Weight vase with gravel to at least one third of its depth. Use plenty of large mesh wire-netting cut slightly more than twice the depth of the unshingled portion and a little wider than the vase. Fold in a U and insert with cut ends uppermost. Pull these up to support fine stems.

2 Preserved leaves, larch cones and iris seedpods define height; graceful beech sprays and hydrangea clusters provide good balance. Preserve leaves by mixing one part glycerine and three parts boiling water, and insert stems in 2 in (5 cm) of the hot solution. Hydrangeas can be treated this way once the bracts colour and texture changes.

3 Use the graceful and delicate perpetuelles for sketching in the outline of arrangement. Stems need not penetrate far into the vase so long as they are firmly held in netting. Chinese lantern-like plant is nicandra. Graceful 'lily' clusters are iris seedpods. Wheat and all farm cereals are well worth using. Gather them green.

Summer Captured

A trug full of self-coloured perpetuelles mixed with colourful helichrysums and physalis, or Chinese lanterns

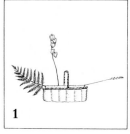

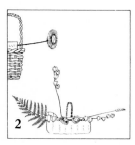

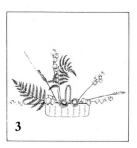

1 Baskets make good containers for dried flower arrangements and there is little danger of knocking them over. To contain fragments of materials loosened by arrangement, baskets need lining. Some can be bought ready lined with tin but cooking foil or polythene may also be used. Cut a block of foamed plastic to fit tightly or, alternatively, use wire-netting.

2 After defining height and general style, decide how low and how far out the shortest stems should flow. Here is a good opportunity to use the short curving-stemmed, larger flowers. Wired stems should be bent so that the flowers flow out nicely. Arrange unwired stems at an angle.

3 Spikes, racemes and studded stems look well in silhouette. The physalis-like nicandra, though not so brilliantly coloured, has a lovely form and habit. Stems of the larger physalis, Chinese lanterns, are cut in sections and the lanterns arranged lower down in ones and twos later.

Autumn Mist

Grasses and thuja form a dainty outline to this medley of greens and greys

1 Fix a block of foamed plastic in a heavy vase. See that it fits quite firmly and let it project a little above rim level so as to give extra height to the perpetuelles. Stems do not need to penetrate far into the foamed plastic to hold firm, but insert the tallest stems the deepest.

2 Many conifers, like the thuja used here, dry well. Divide stems to get dainty sprays. Lengthen stems if necessary by using a double florists' wire or by splicing the stem to a slender twig. Arrange stems at the back first to define height.

3 Make a general outline with graceful tapering materials like the wheat and briza grasses. To give a graceful effect, let drooping tips be silhouetted slightly away from the main bulk of material. Gourds are mounted on wires, the ends being heated before insertion.

Festive Flowers

Creative flower arrangers are so fortunate because they can use their talents to celebrate all manner of festivities, great or small, with floral offerings of their own devising. At first perhaps this may be nothing more novel than a lovingly prepared arrangement of choice or home-grown flowers to mark a birthday. But inevitably there comes a time when the truly creative feel the urge to break away from the expected to produce something more unconventional, or an arrangement that has a touch of wonder. Such an urge is usually prompted by the nature of the festival itself: an Easter decoration prompts the use of eggs, a silver wedding presentation needs silver flowers or their equivalent, a valentine should have a heart or two and a birthday or retirement arrangement for a man is likely to make more impact if it is designed around one of his interests, such as fishing, golf, darts, or maybe some other hobby. All of these, and so many other occasions, set the creative pulse racing.

To achieve the most successful results the arranger may need sometimes to resort to simple floristry, but in the main it should be sufficient merely to be even more liberal in one's approach to design and content than one has learned to be for everyday flower arrangement.

Use artistic licence freely. Follow the basic rules, for these always ease the process of

Summer Wedding – *hollyhocks, petunias, sweet peas, roses and pelargoniums in a white urn raised on an upturned bowl*

arrangement, but bend them constantly.

If choice blooms are scarce or prohibitive in price there are always suitable substitutes to be found and these will gain by being treated as flowers. You can always use fresh foliage or mingled perhaps with a few real flowers as the basic shape, and then embroider it in any way that appeals to you, or which you think will appeal to the person you have in mind. I have used brightly-coloured cotton reels mounted on strong false stems as centres for 'roses' made from skeins of embroidery silks; miniature bottles of liqueur as centres for gold doiley 'sunflowers', white lacey doiley 'arum lilies' wrapped cone-wise around cigars; prettily coloured handkerchiefs gathered to look like blossom and attached to bare beech branches; plastic pastry cutters with laurel leaf 'petals' around them; washing up mops arranged formally with foliage like shaggy chrysanthemums; lollipops and foil-wrapped cookies; mixing bowls filled with fresh herbs and wooden spoon 'flowers'. To make these, stick an attractive cake paper or waxed pudding case behind each spoon with an adhesive, which can be easily wiped off.

Following the same liberal theme, containers to hold festive flowers can be as simply pretty or as outrageous as you wish. Cheap but well-shaped vessels such as stone jam or pickle jars can always be gaily patterned with sequins or coloured paper cut out shapes. Brightly patterned coffee mugs are good holders for flowers. You can find colours or patterns to suit all seasons and to harmonise with the flowers they hold. We have seen in another chapter how well tankards look when filled with flowers. Use these too when you give flowers to men. Many kitchen vessels are not only well designed and suitable for flowers or plants, but they are also acceptable gifts in themselves as well as being suitable for both sexes.

Whether planning New Baby celebration flowers or Diamond Weddings, the arranger will discover that there are so many vessels more suited to the spirit of the occasion than the average vase. Bear in mind that foamed plastic stem holders and waterproof, protective kitchen foil or film enable you to adopt and adapt objects which were never intended in the first place to hold flowers in water.

From selecting one vessel we turn to assembling composite containers, to suit a special purpose. The arrangement 'Table Decoration' (page 149) shows how it is possible to use more than one vessel to create an interesting effect. All kinds of high-rise flower towers can be assembled using this and similar methods. In some, tiers of fruit, or snippets of foliage, or round tree baubles, or fir cones, or what you will can alternate with the flowers.

Flower pots of graduating sizes are also good supports for a tower of graduating bowls. Cake boards or shallow sandwich cake tins can be used successfully for lightweight, out-of-water materials.

It is possible to buy little footed bowls, known as candle cups, which individually fit into the socket of a candlestick and thus convert it into an attractive pedestal 'vase'. These cups and others similar in design sold by some flower-arranger sundriesmen can be used other than in candlesticks. For instance, they can convert a bottle, a tall slim vase, even a piece of thick bamboo cane or copper piping into a useful container. Some arrangers like to use statuettes to hold flowers aloft and these little cups can be fitted into or taped onto the raised hand.

If you wish to arrange fresh flowers with a gift, or perhaps around a bottle of wine, one should be kept separate from the other. Moist foamed plastic is easily isolated if it is wrapped in double kitchen foil. Alternatively you can stand it in a little supplementary container, a margarine tub for instance.

The arrangement 'Easter Morning' (page 148) shows a way of supporting eggs to keep them dry and well apart from the flowers. This same method can be used for other items, as can blocks of dry foamed plastic, as described in the chapter on Flowers and Fruits.

Perhaps it is at Christmas that the creative flower arranger is most busy or has most calls upon his or her time. There are effective short cuts which can be helpful. In the arrangement 'Christmas Story' (page 153) a Christmas tree motif is used. This is one on which limitless themes can be played. Basically one selects a good branch of spruce which resembles the shape of a flat tree. By using a branch as a background for an arrangement of flowers, berries and/or baubles, you not only save a great deal of time, but because of the nature of the evergreen you immediately strike the right seasonal note. Sometimes a branch needs a little grooming, for instance some laterals might flow outwards instead of sideways, or they may cover others. These can be neatly cut off and arranged lower down, or they can be set aside for another decoration.

Branches like this make delightful Christmas trees and take up much less space than real trees. With decorations fastened to the ends of the branches and a group of Christmassy objects, cones, berries, baubles, stars, what you will, at the centre at rim level, this makes a charming decoration which is also just the thing to use as a gift for someone. These can be arranged in flower pots. Alternatively, many glazed pottery kitchen basins and pots look attractive filled this way and, of course, they add to the value of the gift.

The use of these branches need not be confined to the vertical, for from them you can quickly and easily make table decorations or a 'welcome' decoration for your door. For each decoration you need the tips of two well-shaped branches, but do not cut them until you have gauged what their length should be. Begin by laying them flat on a table with their tips pointing in opposite directions. Their

Place two spruce branches end to end. Lash the lower few inches of their stems together side by side, neatly and firmly

stem ends should lie side by side, touching, with the lowest lateral masking the join. Cut as required and tie the stems together, passing the string around the main stems and between the lowest laterals so that they are not tied in to the stems but are well spread out.

Take a small roll of wire netting or a block of foamed plastic and tie it to the centre. If candles are to be used they should be arranged next. Hold these erect in the netting as you arrange the first stems near them. As the stem ends cross they will help wedge the candles in place.

Contrary to the method followed when arranging fresh flowers, it is best not to strip the stem ends of the basic evergreens used this way. The decorative materials used later may have to have their stem ends stripped and cut on a slant in some cases so that they can be easily inserted among those used as the foundation.

Fix a roll of wire netting to the centre, over the tied stems. See that all lies flat and firm. The candles are placed in position next. Short stems of spruce and other evergreens are then pushed in horizontally to wedge the candles firmly in place

Decorations can be long and oval in shape, the stems which give width to the arrangement being much shorter than those which define the length. To make a circular decoration, arrange stems of fairly equal length at the very base of the netting roll. These should lie flat on the table.

Work from the base upwards, gradually altering the angle of the stems so that they lie almost flat at first, gradually leaning at a smaller angle until they become almost upright by the time they are grouped at the centre. None should stretch out beyond the basic stems arranged initially.

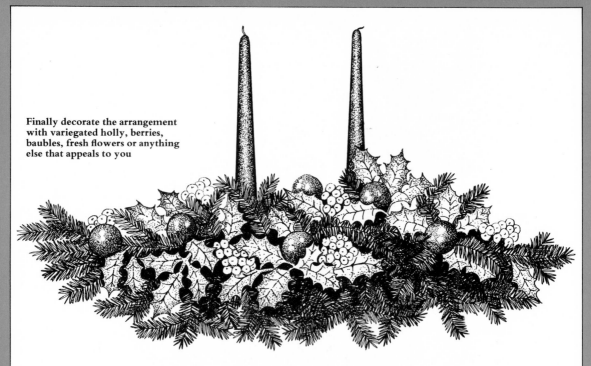

Finally decorate the arrangement with variegated holly, berries, baubles, fresh flowers or anything else that appeals to you

Once an attractive dense background has been made of the plain green, add some more decorative foliage such as variegated holly, ivy, euonymus, elaeagnus or a golden conifer of some kind, whatever you can find that looks well. Arrange sprigs of berried holly separately, after you have carefully cut off the leaves with scissors. This way you get full colour value.

This type of arrangement can be placed on a flat dish or raised on a comport or cake stand once it is completed.

You can adapt this method of construction to make a 'welcome' decoration for a door. You can keep the rounded outline so that it is somewhat garland-shaped, or as a contrast you can set out to make everything much more informal, using longer, slender stems at the edges with some ivy trails perhaps, and maybe pendent cones hung on ribbons and a bell or two.

If you are always prepared to adapt patterns you know well you will always have something new to make. For instance, 'Golden Anniversary' (page 147) shows a little tree made of dried materials. It is possible to make the same kind of decoration using fresh flowers. These make delightful gifts (try one for the new baby) as well as novel table or buffet decorations. Little rose trees are pretty at weddings. A double daisy tree will delight a child. Christmas and winter trees can be made from evergreens, berries and everlastings. You can make trees for a buffet supper from bay and other herbs and decorate with lemons or bright capsicum fruits. Lollipop trees will be fun for a children's party table.

One practical note; to keep the plastic foundation from slipping down the trunk, twist a rubber band three or four times around it immediately below the plastic.

Golden Anniversary

Gilded, dried Chiffon roses and Lonicera nitida *in a gilded flower pot*

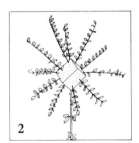

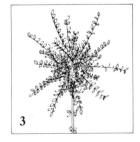

1 Say it with flowers that will keep long after The Day is over. Weight a plastic flower pot or cream carton with a pebble on each side of the centre. Top with a block of foamed plastic. Pass a trimmed twig of lonicera (or box) down through the foam and between the pebbles to the base of the pot. Cut a cube of foamed plastic or use a specially manufactured plastic globe, and fix on top of the 'stem'.

2 Cut lonicera into 3-in (8-cm) lengths. Stud these all over the foundation. Cut shorter lengths and recess them to hide the foam (see drawing below). Only a short portion of each stem need be inserted. Dry roses by hanging them upside down in an airing cupboard. Many kinds are suitable, so experiment first to find which do best.

3 Cut the rose stems a little longer than the lonicera, and strip off faded leaves. When inserting the stems, hold them low down and push firmly. Finally, spray all over arrangement and container with gold paint, except for one or two leaves which should be left green.

147

Easter Morning

Apple blossom and coloured eggs in a basket

1 Find a bowl of the same depth as the basket and big enough to hold a large pinholder and water. Alternatively, use a large potato, take a slice off the base so it stands firm and wedge it inside the bowl. Fill the remaining area in the basket with large mesh wire-netting pushed right up against its sides to hold the bowl firm.

2 Cut the base of the blossom branch on the slant so that it can be easily impaled on the pinholder or stuck in the potato. Trim away any ungainly or unwanted side stems. Cut off all dead shoots or damaged leaves. Arrange some of the lower stems but do not cover the pinholder yet.

3 Cover wire-netting with moss or something similar. This should be dry to stop the colours of the eggs running. Press the surface down – the netting provides nice hollows to hold the eggs safely. Arrange these round the rim of the basket first, then pile more on top. Finally hide the holder with blossom and dot more small sprigs among the eggs.

148

Table Decoration

Carnations and roses in tiered bowls

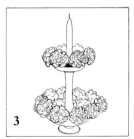

1 Any kind of round flower can be used for an arrangement of this type. The 'vase' is made from a bowl, a candlestick and a candle cup holder. If the candlestick does not stand quite firm, place four small pills of plasticine or adhesive clay on the dry base and press down onto the dry bowl.

2 Fill the lower bowl with a ring of wire-netting or, alternatively, pack it with foamed plastic. If the pinholder in the top bowl has no centre well for the candle, heat it with hot water so that the candle slips on to the warm points. Allow water to cool before arranging any flowers.

3 Arrange outer rings of flowers first. Rest the blooms on the rims of the bowls to face outwards. In this way they will give greater colour value. An outer ring of attractive leaves could be used instead of flowers. Finally arrange the inner rings.

149

Hearts and Flowers

'My love's like a red, red rose,' could be said to be the theme of this Valentine arrangement. Emphasis has been laid equally on the choice of flowers and their colour. The fragrant freesias contribute a little floral gold to harmonise with the doiley 'lace' below them.

Shiny new baking tins, rectangular or round, make excellent containers for certain festive occasions. Christmas greens and bright red berries, for instance, contrast beautifully with the silvery effect of, say, a new, long gingerbread tin. Use them for table arrangements on a grand scale, for they sit nicely along the centre, as they do on church windowsills for Harvest and Flower Festival arrangements. However, there are occasions when the tin is best covered, as with this Valentine gift, where the rich red and gold cover hints of Victoriana.

Crepe paper was chosen as the tin cover because it is elastic and can easily be draped over rounded shapes. A square of this was cut, a dab of quick-drying adhesive applied to the centre and the heart-shaped tin stood on it. The purpose of the adhesive is simply to hold

the paper securely in place as its edges are pulled over the sides. These were then drawn into the centre, flattened down and once again touched with adhesive to keep them in place.

The doiley, being round, had to be folded here and there so that it fitted well inside the heart-shaped outline.

Next the container for the block of foamed plastic was put in place. This was a small waterproof waxed paper dish, the kind sold in packets for party foods. Adhesive was applied to its base so that it would remain in place when transported. Flowers and ribbons were then arranged so that they remained within the heart shape.

Fix a waxed paper dish (the sort of thing jellies are served in at children's parties) to the floor of the crepe paper-covered heart with quick-drying adhesive

Cut a block of foamed plastic to fit into the base of the dish. Soak well before placing it in position. Insert the stems of the roses firmly into the sides of the plastic

A heart-shaped baking tin holds red roses, fragrant freesias and scented pelargonium leaves.

New Baby

Miniature roses, spiraea, lobelia, alyssum, candytuft, field daisies, herb Robert, in a tiny Dresden cup and saucer

1 Welcome a new arrival, boy or girl, with a treasure scaled to size. Many little antique pieces make perfect containers for miniature flower arrangements. For safety's sake, the cup can be anchored to the saucer with transparent adhesive tape. The flowers should hide most of this.

2 If the flowers are cut short and massed together, you will not need a stem holder. If, however, the present has to be moved, fill the bottom half of the container with a piece of foamed plastic. Arrange the firm-stemmed roses first.

3 Once in place, the roses will hold firm the more delicate stems of the other flowers. Arrange tiny fern-like leaves (herb Robert in our picture) over the rim to frame the little blooms. See that only the stem of the leaf is in the water or it may act as a siphon.

Christmas Story

Seasonal spruce with starry anemone-centred chrysanthemums, side stems from a spray and holly berries with ivy

1

1 Spruce branches closely resemble the shape of the Christmas tree from which they are cut. The tip cut from a branch is arranged right at the back of a simple container filled with large mesh wire-netting to make a tree-like framework for the flowers and berries. Netting ends are hooked round the stem at rim level.

2

2 Side stems from the rest of the branch are arranged at the foot of the 'tree'. An inch or two (3 to 5 cm) of the main stem is cut with each piece so that it flows nicely out at right angles to the main stem. Bring these stems forward.

3

3 Grade the chrysanthemums so that the longest stem, and, if there is a variation in size, the smallest bloom is at the top of the curve. Place them back as near to the branch as possible to leave room for the thicker holly stems. Leaves are carefully cut from berry sprigs.

153

Christmas Tree

Yellow and white statice, honesty glittered briza grasses and baubles in a white urn

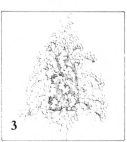

1 Cut a block of foamed plastic into roughly a cone-shape or use a specially manufactured plastic cone. Alternatively, take three or more cylinders and stack them on top of one another and top with a half cylinder. Join these together by passing a slim cane right down through the centre to the base of the container.

2 Divide stems of statice to make short-stemmed sprigs. Keep shorter lengths for the top of the cone. Arrange the longest stems low with their tips pointing downwards. As you arrange the shorter stems, point them downwards if they are in the centre or upwards if they are at the tip.

3 Fill the spaces between the statice with shorter stems of honesty and briza which should hang down prettily. Finally, decorate with baubles. These should be mounted on pipe cleaners (passed through the small circle of wire from which each one hangs).

Index